The Practical Guide to Craft Bookbinding

THE PRACTICAL GUIDE TO *Craft*

ARTHUR W. JOHNSON

Bookbinding

With 128 illustrations

THAMES AND HUDSON

Printed and bound in the German Democratic Republic

Contents

Introduction

how to use this book

The aim of this book is to explain, by means of theory, general instruction and progressive exercises, the principles by which books are constructed. In addition, the projects in Part II are planned so that the beginner will acquire hand skills in order to practise the craft either professionally or as a serious pastime. The information will also benefit librarians, collectors, booksellers and anyone who is concerned with and sympathetic to books and bindings.

Much of the instruction is concerned with theory, as binding books without understanding the reasons for the processes is a sterile occupation. Thus the book not only includes projects explaining the techniques step by step – and which are designed to produce completed bindings (Part II, pp.59-87) – but also chapters on the theory of the many operations and general instruction for executing them (Part I, Chapters 1-12). The reader is urged to study Part I carefully as an aid to perfecting the projects.

Binding a book involves a series of operations that relate to each other and which must be followed with care. These operations are listed in detail at the end of each project, both as an aid to carrying out the project and also for revision purposes. They fall into two categories: 'forwarding' and 'finishing'. Forwarding is the production of the binding itself and is the source of the book's strength and durability. It involves taking the book apart ('pulling'), repairing damaged leaves, pressing, making the endpapers, sewing the sections of the text paper together, cutting the edges, shaping the spine ('rounding and backing'), preparing boards for front and back, making the headbands (reinforcements, usually decorative, for the top and bottom of the spine), strengthening the spine with linings of mull and brown paper, paring the leather for the cover, covering the boards with leather or cloth, covering the exposed parts of the boards with cloth or paper if appropriate ('siding') and pasting down the endpapers. Finishing is the art of lettering and decorating the cover. The Working Procedures (Chapters 5-12) deal with the basic operations that apply to most of the projects in Part II. They follow the order in which they are done in practice. Both forwarding and finishing require much skill and imagination, and each is dependent on the other for the accomplishment of a binding which is at once functional and aesthetically pleasing.

Although much can be learnt from textbooks, there are innumerable practical tips, methods, equipment modifications and short cuts that can only be learnt from a teacher. Moreover, dubious practices, theories and surmises may confuse the beginner, so it is highly recommended to attend classes and benefit from demonstrations and lectures by teachers proficient in the craft. (See list of schools on p.93.) The student should always be discriminate and follow only those methods that can be backed by sound scientific principles and common sense.

It is at first puzzling to discover that in this exacting craft no measuring takes place, for distances and proportions should be judged by eye. An efficient bookbinder wastes no time in taking measurements from a ruler. Nevertheless, measurements are given in this book as a guide for the beginner. The student should be familiar with millimetre readings so that, with practice, distances may be assessed accurately.

For a complete appreciation of the craft, students should concern themselves with all aspects of book production, and a study of the manufacture and suitability of paper, the methods of printing, lettering, typography and the reproduction of illustrations, is essential. Ability and understanding will increase with a knowledge of the history of book construction and decoration, and of the history, manufacture and use of tools and materials. The list of further reading on p.96 will guide the reader as to the best sources to consult.

It should be noted that although the word 'elementary' is often used when beginning the craft, this is for want of a more suitable term. The craft itself cannot be labelled elementary, since even the first exercises require skills that will challenge a creative person. This fascinating craft will, I hope, open up vast areas of interest and give much enjoyment and personal satisfaction in the creation of bindings which preserve the contents of the book, please the eye and are a joy to possess.

Part One

Forwarding

1 Work space, tools and equipment

Any room in a house will serve as a bindery, but outhouses, tool sheds, cellars and garages are unsuitable because of humidity, temperature and insect pests. There should be good light by day, and strip lighting that will not cast shadows over the working area. An adjustable bench light is necessary for detailed work. A first aid box, waste bin and broom should be provided, and overalls worn. Benches and heavy equipment should be positioned at right angles to floor joists. Work tops can be constructed from 4 × 4 in. (10 × 10 cm) timber, or from a braced framework of Dexion, surfaced with 20mm chipboard and further covered with vinyl floor covering, the plain side up. A bench 35 in. wide, 60 in. long and 35 in. high (90 × 158 × 90 cm) is ideal. Cupboards and shelving for the storage of paper, board and materials can be built under the benches. A high stool is essential. A separate bench, close to the others and strong enough for the nipping press (see below), should be constructed with space at the side for books being forwarded and with racks beneath for pressing, cutting and backing boards. All work tops should be 'fenced' with 2 in. (5 cm) wooden battens to prevent tools falling off. All wooden parts of equipment should be rubbed·over periodically with wax furniture polish or linseed oil.

Heavy equipment

It is important for the beginner to learn with professional equipment. 'Junior' models make the acquisition of skills difficult and frustrating. (Edge cutting, for example, will be inaccurate and the size of books limited.)

Lying (laying) press (1). An essential item of equipment which is used for cutting books and boards, backing, pressing and finishing. This press, whose design has not changed for 500 years, is of beech with massive wooden screws capable of tremendous pressure and of holding large volumes. The professional size is not less than 24 in. (61 cm) between the screws. Some modern presses have iron screws with a centre wheel for adjusting the distance between the blocks of the press (the 'cheeks'). It is supported on a stand or 'tub', and the worker should be able to move around it freely. One end of the tub has its legs sloping inwards, so that the worker can stand without hindrance and lean over the press. Two hooks screwed to the side of the tub hold the press pin, which is used to adjust the pressure.

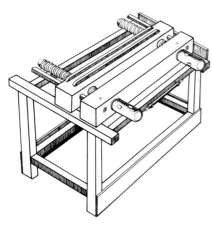

1. Lying press, tub and press pin

8

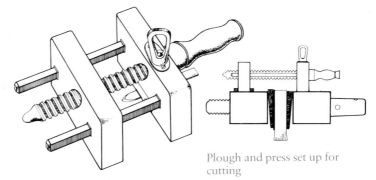

2. Plough

Plough and press set up for cutting

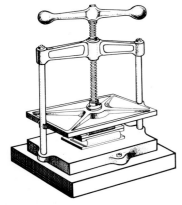

3. Nipping press

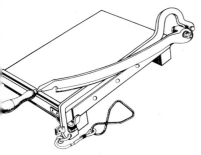

4. Board chopper

5. Sewing frame and tape keys

Light equipment

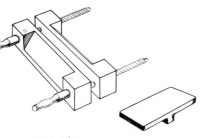

Plough (2). This is used for cutting book edges and boards. It is pushed along the runners on the lying press.

Nipping press (3). This is an essential piece of equipment and is used for a wide variety of tasks: to press books to reduce their bulk, for the making of endpapers, etc. The larger the press, the more efficient it is, but an adequate size is 15 × 20 in. (38 × 51 cm), with a maximum of 14 in. (35 cm) between the base and top plates. The base plate should be lined with a piece of card the same size and marked with diminishing rectangles as a guide to positioning books at the centre of the press and thereby obtaining even pressure.

Board chopper (cutter) (4). Used for cutting paper and board. It has a scissor action and is fitted with a clamp to hold the work firmly in position. The one illustrated has a 24 in. (61 cm) blade and an adjustable stirrup clamp, although there are many satisfactory models available. When the blades become blunt, they should be sharpened and set professionally.

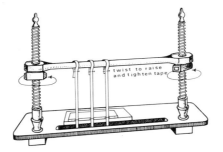

twist to raise and tighten tape

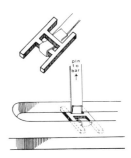

pin to bar

Sewing frame and six tape-sewing keys (5). The frame is used for both tape and cord sewing. A maximum of 20 in. (51 cm) between the screws is adequate for most work.

Finishing press (6). A small bench press used for holding books while lettering, and lining the spines. It should measure 15 in. (38 cm) between the screws.

Knocking-down iron (7). This is used for specific operations in both elementary and advanced bookbinding, and also as a weight. Size: about 10 × 25 cm.

6. Finishing press
7. Knocking-down iron

9

8. Electric gluepot

Sundries

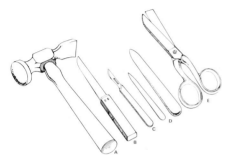

9. Backing hammer, cobbler's knife, scalpel, bone folders, shears

10. Cutting boards (A) and backing boards (B)

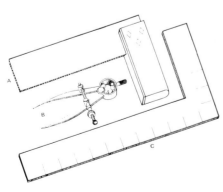

11. Carpenter's square, engineer's dividers, leather square

Electric gluepot (8). The safest type has a waterless jacket and is thermostatically controlled.

Paring stone (55). A slab of Bavarian limestone used for paring leather and as a surface for covering books. A good size is 35 × 51 cm. A piece of marble or polished slate is cheaper but equally serviceable.

These are numerous and depend on how seriously the craft is to be practised. The essentials are as follows:

Backing hammer (9A). Weighing 1 lb., with a domed head and a claw.

Cobbler's knife (**utility knife**) (9B). A wooden-handled knife for rough cutting.

Scalpel (9C). Handle with a replaceable blade; used for accurate cutting.

Oilstone. Coarse grit on one side and fine on the other; used for sharpening tools. This should be fixed in a box, so that it does not come into contact with paper.

Two bone folders (**folding sticks**) (9D). The larger should be 175mm long with a thick, rounded base and a shaped point suitable for all work. The smaller should be 112mm long and finely pointed for use in the finishing processes.

Shears (9E). Blunt ended, 225mm long; used for tough materials.

Ordinary scissors for accurate cutting.

Cutting boards (10A). Pairs of wedge-shaped boards of beech with the wide end at right angles to one of the sides. Used in the cutting of book edges. The three pairs should be 225, 300 and 375mm long, and about 125mm wide.

Backing boards (10B). Three pairs of wedge-shaped boards for shaping the spine ('backing'; 48). They must not be confused with cutting boards; the wide ends are cut to an angle of 115 degrees to one side. These boards should be the same sizes as the cutting boards.

Carpenter's square (**right-angle gauge**) (11A) with a 225mm blade.

Engineer's dividers (11B). These should measure about 150mm and have their points blunted to avoid scratching the material.

Leather square (11C).

45-degree set square.

Tenon saw with fine teeth; used for cutting a channel ('cerf') into the folds of the sections before sewing. (A fine hacksaw will serve as well.)

Loaded stick for beating the swell out of the backs of the sections while sewing. Made from a piece of wood 250 × 25 × 25mm, with a piece of lead attached to one end and bound with leather.

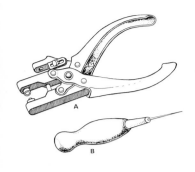

12. Hole punch/eyeletting pliers and bodkin

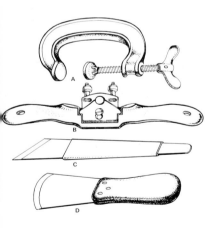

13. Leather-paring tools: G clamp, spokeshave, English and French paring knives

Combined hole punch and eyeletting pliers (12A) with a supply of coloured eyelets.

Small bookbinding bodkin (12B) for piercing holes in paper and board.

Strop. Made as follows: shape the first 125mm of a piece of flat wood 50 × 450mm into a handle, and glue onto the remainder a strip of medium emery cloth on one side and a thick piece of hide on the other. Coat the hide with tallow and sprinkle it with emery dust. Apply a hot iron until the tallow melts and carries the dust into the grain of the leather. (Valve grinding compound can be a substitute for tallow and emery; this is simply smeared on.)

Two glue bushes, 25 and 51mm (16). The hairs are bound with wire to make them stiff.

Two paste brushes with unbound hairs, 25 and 51mm (16).

Bristle nail brush.

Wood chisel, 12mm, for rounding corners of boards and cutting slots for portfolio ties.

Two steel straight-edges, 305mm and 610mm, ruled in inches and millimetres, for cutting out materials.

Three pairs of pressing boards. Made from ply board or formica-faced chipboard. The following sizes are the most useful: 150 × 225, 225 × 300, 300 × 450mm.

Sanding blocks and sticks. Made from pieces of wood or flat battens to which are glued strips of sandpaper of coarse and fine grits.

Bookbinders' needles of various sizes.

Pair of knitting needles or similar rods of stainless steel, wood or plastic, 4mm in diameter. (Iron should not be used, as it will turn wet leather black.)

Two G clamps (13A), 100mm, for use in paring leather.

Spokeshave (13B). A carpenter's tool adopted successfully by the bookbinder for paring leather. Obtain one with an adjustable blade, and flat (not convex) on the under side. The tool must be modified for bookbinding by filing the blade slot wider to free the leather shavings, and by shaping the blade edge into a gentle curve so that paring occurs in the centre of the blade.

Paring knives. If possible the student should try both the English (13C) and French knife (13D) to find the one most suited. Generally the former is popular and can be obtained for both left- and right-handed people. A strip of leather pasted round the handle will prevent sore fingers.

For ease of access to these tools, a piece of ply board can be screwed to the wall within reach of the work space, with hooks and clips on which all these small tools may be hung.

11

Safety

Protruding parts of equipment must be padded. Points and edges of sharp tools should be corked or kept in sheaths when not in use. Keep the board chopper blade down and avoid striking metal against metal. Be cautious with flammable materials and keep them in metal cupboards if possible. Service electrical equipment regularly. If weights are made from bricks or lead, cover them and devise some form of carrying handle.

Sharpening knives

Keep all knives sharp: a blunt blade is more likely to slip and cause damage when pressure is applied.

The cobbler's knife. An instant keen edge is achieved by holding the blade almost flat on the emery side of the strop and beating along the length with a bias of pressure at the edge. Sharpen both sides of the blade. The blade should be shaped as in 14A, since cutting is achieved by slicing through with the curve.

The plough blade is shaped as illustrated in 14B and C and sharpened on the bevelled edge, never on the flat side, or imperfect cutting will result. The bevel is held against the oilstone and long figure-of-eight movements are made first on one side of the bevel then on the other, to the full length of the stone (14C). Raising the blade alternately left and right on the return movement will preserve the spear shape. A final beating of the two edges on the leather strop will make them keen.

Paring knives are sharpened only on the bevelled side. (Any change on the flat side will make paring impossible.) Hold the bevel against the surface of the stone and push backwards and forwards to its full length, without alteration to the angle (14D). Finally use the leather strop as before.

Spokeshave blades and French knives are sharpened in the same way as the plough blade.

It is likely in all cases that a burr, or lip of metal, will occur on the flat side. This is removed by 'wiping' this side firmly, flat on the surface of the oilstone. With constant sharpening the bevels become reduced and it will be necessary to regrind.

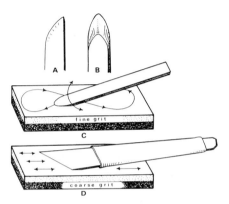

14. Knife sharpening: A, cobbler's knife; B, C, plough blade; D, English paring knife

2
Materials

Manufactured materials of all kinds vary in their acidity or alkalinity, but those used for bookbinding should be as near neutral as possible for them to be durable. They are measured on a pH scale ('power of hydrogen ions') from 0 to 14, neutral being 7. Acidic solutions and materials have pH values below 7, and alkaline ones above. The scale is logarithmic: i.e. 6 is ten times as acidic as 7, 5 a hundred times, 4 a thousand times, and so on. Acid and alkaline materials are the chief causes of deterioration of books and documents, and the process is further accelerated by the absorption of the industrial atmosphere. For instance, some newsprint is 4.5 (highly acidic) on the pH scale and therefore deteriorates rapidly; it is also detrimental to anything in close proximity to it. The pH value must be considered when choosing all materials. A piece of leather from an old handbag used for a book cover, or wallpaper for endpapers, will make an unsound binding, as both may be acidic.

In general, imitation materials are to be avoided, as, for example, sheep leather stamped to look like pigskin, paper embossed to look like linen, and cheap bookcloth finished to simulate expensive buckram. Their use is dishonest and unworthy of fine bookbinding. The materials listed below are standard and are used for the projects in Part II.

Leather   This is used for durable and fine book coverings.

Morocco (goatskin) is the most popular leather. It owes its durability to the fact that it is tanned with oak bark or sumach. It is produced under many trade names, but should always have a stamp or label on the back stating that it has passed the PIRA test. (This test, instigated by the Printing Industries Research Association, guarantees that the leather has been manufactured without the aid of injurious acids; see pH Values, above.) Unstamped leather should not be used, especially leather with a cellulose dressing, as difficulty may be experienced in working and finishing. Skins are sold as 'footage' and the size is marked on the back. For example, the figure 6 followed by a small 1 is 6¼ square feet; 6 followed by a small 2 is 6½; and 6 followed by a small 3 is 6¾. All binding leather is of the same basic quality but skins are graded 'A' (firsts or best), 'B' (seconds) and 'C' (thirds), according to faults such as scars, holes and uneven dyeing. The price per foot is adjusted accordingly. (A 'B' skin is perfectly satisfactory for general bookbinding, even with a few marks — indeed, as today's plastics can easily be mistaken for

13

perfect leather, a few blemishes help to distinguish the genuine article.) The compressed thickness after processing can be as little as one millimetre, although the skin appears thicker because of the bulky fibre. Thicker leather is obtained from the hides of mountain goats and is known as Levant morocco; this should only be used for larger bindings where extra strength is required. Moroccos are popular for their beautiful range of colours which are fast and work well in the covering process. The leather sticks well with paste, is flexible, of good appearance, pares without difficulty and is very receptive to gold tooling (see p. 53). As it is a natural substance, it has no grain and pieces can be cut economically from any part, and from any direction. The flank, however, is avoided for fine work as it stretches when pared; the neck is hard, thick and difficult to thin down. In general, skins with a well-defined, textured surface should be chosen.

Calfskin. A popular leather of earlier times, when its warm brown colour recommended it for institutional and private libraries. Its smooth surface can be delicately and intricately tooled with gold leaf. Tastes have now changed, however, and more colourful leathers are in demand. Skins are larger than moroccos and range from thin calf to thick, soft, tanned hides from older animals. It is not as durable as morocco and is used chiefly for the restoration of old and facsimile bindings.

Cloth

This is used for economy bindings. It should always be cut so that the warp thread runs from the top to the bottom of the book. This warp, which is the equivalent of the grain direction in paper, is readily identifiable as it is parallel to the selvedges and will tear easily in a straight line. The price of the cloth denotes its quality. (High quality cloth is not necessarily suitable for all bookbinding as it is often hard and stiff, and should not be used for small books, as it does not fold easily.)

Buckram. A strong, closely woven cloth of linen or linen/cotton mixture, with a natural finish. Some types are treated on the back with a pigment 'filler' such as china clay, or are backed with tissue paper, to prevent glue penetrating during work, and the surface may be matt, or glazed to resist marks and moisture. It is used for medium-sized and large books and boxes, where appearance and strength are important. A wide range of colours and textures is available.

Bookcloth. Woven from cotton fibres, bookcloth is backed with pigment or paper. It is used for economical bindings, small books and boxes. It varies considerably in price, quality, colour and finish.

Jaconette. An open-weave white cotton cloth heavily impregnated with a starch filler to facilitate handling and prevent glue penetration. Used for strengthening endpapers, book joints, spines, sections, plates, and for lining maps.

Mull (super). An open-weave cotton cloth, with the warp and weft threads clearly defined. Like jaconette, it is stiffened with starch. The thinner, cheaper ranges have little strength, but the better quality is used for lining spines and as hinges for ephemeral bindings. On its own it is weak, but reinforces anything to which it is stuck.

Rexine (leather cloth). This is made by spreading a mixture of alcohol, cellulose nitrate and camphor oil onto a cloth backing. Being an imitation of leather, it is sometimes regarded as a second-rate material, but it is highly recommended for children's books, cooking and gardening reference books, portfolios and nautical chart cases as it is impervious to moisture and will stand hard use. It may be satisfactorily gold tooled with foil.

Plastic fabrics

This term covers many types of paper or cloth surfaced or impregnated with plastic. They have advantages over other materials as they are cheap, waterproof and not easily stained. They are, however, little used by craft binders because of their imitative appearance. (Firms producing diaries, Bibles and wedding albums where a convincing imitation of leather is required make frequent use of them.)

Board

Board is tested for grain direction by holding opposite edges and bending the board, then repeating with the other two edges. The 'bend' that is least resistant to pressure is the grain direction. This being confirmed, it should be indicated by drawing a number of parallel lines on the board with a pencil, thus making it unnecessary to test the same piece of board every time.

Strawboard. Manufactured from straw fibre imported from Holland, it is used for economical bindings and for boxes. It is very durable but tends to be brittle. Like paper (see p. 20), it is measured in grams per square metre, ranging from 500 gsm to 1000, 1400, 1800 gsm and above.

Greyboard. A pale grey board which is rather soft; an inferior substitute for strawboard. It tends to be acidic, as it is made from indeterminate printing waste. Thickness is measured in decimal sizes: e.g. 1.8mm (thin), 2.33mm (medium) and 3.1mm (heavy).

Millboard. A high quality greyboard, which is durable, hard and has a firm surface. It ranges in colour from light grey or greenish to dark brown or black. It is made from sisal rope, hemp and jute sack fibre with some printing waste. Its advantage is that it bends

15

without cracking. It is measured in decimal sizes, e.g. 1.6mm (thin), 2.3mm (medium) and 3.2mm (heavy).

Tape This is used to attach the sections to the boards (83). Pure linen tape measuring 12mm wide is standard, although cotton tape may be used for bindings of no particular value.

Thread Unbleached linen thread only is used for book sewing, as it is very strong and durable, and has a neutral pH value (see p.13). Strands are combined to make various thicknesses, which manufacturers number according to their own systems (e.g. one strand of thread is often designated 16, two strands twisted together 16/2, three 16/3).

Thread thickness has, unfortunately, not been standardized, so to recommend particular thicknesses here would be misleading. Thread is available in reels and skeins. The latter are held together with a small loop; the skein should be hooked up by this loop before use, pulled taut and the threads cut through. It is then divided into three and plaited loosely to prevent tangles. Lengths of thread are pulled from the bottom.

Paper Paper is the basic material in bookbinding, and the student should therefore make a study of the different papers and their properties, reaction to adhesives and suitability as to purpose. This knowledge is gained by experience, but the task can be simplified by using a limited range of papers in the early stages. Recommended papers are: drawing cartridge for white endpapers, Abbey Mill antique laid for coloured endpapers in the economical range, and Ingres paper of any shade for better quality bindings. Handmade paper is sold in reams of 480 sheets, quires of 24 sheets, or single sheets. Machine-mades are sold in reams of 500 sheets, quires of 25 sheets, or single sheets.

Handmade paper
Paper made by hand today is expensive. Few mills are in production, and much is imported from Sweden and Japan. A steady demand for prestige printing, art and calligraphy work, however, ensures that the craft of papermaking will continue. Its appeal lies in its permanence, strength and texture. Although a superb material for the bookbinder, its hardness and lack of grain direction may cause difficulty for the beginner, and it is therefore recommended only for advanced work.

The production of handmade paper
The raw materials are linen and cotton, used in proportions according to the hardness of the paper

required: the greater the proportion of linen, the harder the paper. Water is added to the raw material, which is pulped and put into a vat. The papermaker uses a sieve or 'mould', which is a wooden frame with a base of woven wires. There are two types of mould: the 'laid' mould and the 'wove' mould. In the former the warp wires are about 25mm apart and the weft wires close together. In wove moulds both warp, and weft are tightly and regularly spaced. The pattern of laid paper can be observed by holding the paper up to the light. Inside the mould is another wooden frame called a 'deckle', whose depth determines the thickness of the paper and causes the characteristic broken edge (the 'deckle edge'), where fibres creep between the deckle and mould frames. The mould and deckle are put into the vat to scoop up the pulp, lifted out, shaken from left to right, tilted slightly and moved backward and forward to distribute the pulp evenly. The watermark is also impressed, as it is incorporated into the mould as woven wire. As the water escapes, the fibres knit together. Once the sheets are drained, they are placed between blankets or felts and put in piles and pressed. The sheets are then dried and passed through a bath of diluted animal gelatine ('size'). The 'tub sizing' or 'surface sizing' gives strength, finish, permanence and a partial resistance to moisture. Finally the sheets are squeezed and dried in a current of warm air.

The sheets are sorted into 'goods' (perfect sheets) and 'retree' (seconds) according to marks and faults. The surface can be 'rough', 'not' (not glazed) or 'hot pressed' (glazed). Paper is glazed by pressing the paper between hot metal plates which firm and smooth the surface so that it may be used for writing and fine printing. 'Not' is commonly used for fine bookbinding, particularly for endpapers.

Machine-made paper

The raw material is softwood, and the paper produced by two methods: mechanical wood pulping and chemical wood pulping. In the former, the raw wood containing all its impurities, such as lignin, is ground and the fibre extracted. This is then beaten by machine to produce cheap but acidic paper (see pH Values, p.13). (Newsprint, for example, contains 80 per cent mechanical wood pulp, the remainder being sulphite pulp from chemically treated wood.) Without the addition of size, and having a high acid content, this paper rapidly disintegrates with use and weather. However, by treating the pulp with chemicals, paper with a much longer life can be produced. Most paper today, therefore, is made by chemical wood pulping. It ranges in quality from ledger paper, which compares favourably with handmade paper, to the cheapest wrapping paper. The quality is determined by the fibre, the beating treatment, chemical additives, sizing, addition of kaolin ('loading'), and the treatment of the surface ('finishing').

The production of machine-made paper

Wood chips are first disintegrated by caustics to decompose the lignin and reduce the acid content. This material is put in a 'Hydropulper' machine to separate the fibres and then beaten to reduce them so that they bond together more firmly. To the resulting 'stuff' can be added dye, loading (china clay) or size (here termed 'engine sizing' as it is done before the paper is made), according to the type of paper required. (Loading bulks out the paper and makes it more receptive to printing ink for fine colour reproduction. Loaded paper also has greater opacity and can be given a high glaze.) The pulp is spread onto a continuous moving belt of wire or nylon thread (the 'wire part'). As the belt oscillates from side to side, the fibres felt together, tending to lie in the direction the belt is travelling.

The resulting machine direction, or grain, is of the utmost importance to the bookbinder. No binding operations are successful unless the grain in paper, cloth, board, mull and jaconette all run the same way, from the top of the book to the bottom. If conflicting energies occur, boards will warp, endpapers crinkle, joints will split and the book will not close.

The water is sucked out of the pulp while it is moving along the belt. The resulting paper has a 'wove' appearance (see handmade paper); if a 'laid' appearance is required, it then passes, on the belt, under a 'Dandy' roller of woven wire which impresses a pattern like that of handmade laid paper and also, if required, the water-mark. The paper is then pressed and dried. (Some quality writing and drawing papers are tub-sized at this stage, while those intended for fine colour printing receive a coating of china clay rather than being loaded, to make them more receptive to the printing ink. These are known as 'art papers'.) The surface is glazed, polished and firmed as required by calender rollers. The paper is finally reeled and slit to smaller sizes.

If the paper is made by machine in separate sheets rather than reels, it is termed 'mould-made' paper. This is generally made from chemical wood and rag fibres, is well sized and is almost as permanent as handmade paper. Examples are Ingres paper and papers used for archivist restoration. It is expensive.

There are innumerable types of paper used for bookbinding, which can be classified as printings, writings, wrappings, drawings, blottings, handmades and specials. The student should be familiar with all these categories and their properties, so that the correct paper can be chosen for the project in hand.

Paper sizes

Metric measurements have been accepted world wide, but it is still necessary for the craft binder to know the traditional sizes because he or she will be concerned with old books which were made in these sizes. The common ones are:

imperial	30 × 22 in.
royal	25 × 20 in.
medium	23 × 18 in.
demy	22½ × 17½ in.
crown	20 × 15 in.
foolscap	17 × 13½ in.

Larger versions of these sizes are also made: double crown, for example, measures 20 × 30 in. (only the shorter side being doubled), and quad crown 40 × 30 in. (both sides being doubled). Sections of a book (see p.23) are produced by folding the sheets of one of the above sizes, as follows:

crown	20 × 15 in. (1 leaf or 2 pages)
crown folio	15 × 10 in. (2 leaves or 4 pages)
crown quarto	10 × 7½ in. (4 leaves or 8 pages)
crown octavo	7½ × 5 in. (8 leaves or 16 pages)

Seldom is paper folded again, as distortion will occur (thin paper, however, will fold to 32 pages). Although old books were made according to the above paper sizes, measurements may vary because of indiscriminate folding and cutting. If the sheet is folded in half, parallel to the long side, this size is referred to as 'long folio' (e.g. 'crown long folio').

In recent years, the multiplicity of paper sizes throughout the world has needed simplification for the exchange of trade and for the standardization of printing and processing machinery.

The ISO (International Standards Organization) has therefore agreed upon three groups of metric sizes for use world wide: 'A'-size papers for all printed work; 'B'-size papers for posters and wall charts; and 'C' sizes for envelopes and folders (to contain 'A'-sized paper).

A0	1189 × 841mm.
A1 (A0 folded or cut once)	841 × 594mm.
A2 (A0 folded or cut twice)	594 × 420mm.
A3 (A0 folded or cut three times)	420 × 297mm.
A4 (A0 folded or cut four times)	297 × 210mm.
etc.	

This has enabled all printing equipment to be standardized, as all the sheets are of the same proportion. A sheet double the size of AO is designated 2AO, and one four times the size 4AO. If an AO sheet is folded or cut parallel to its longer side, it is designated A1L. The above measurements refer to the finished size after folding and cutting, which obviates any deviations caused by different methods of print production. Paper intended for books is sold in slightly larger sheets to allow for processing and trimming of the pages: these are termed RAO, and the sheet measures 1220 × 860mm. Paper intended for book covers also has to be larger to allow for subsequent processing. It is designated SRAO, and the sheet measures 1280 × 900mm.

A further complication arises in that certain traditional English book sizes have been retained, but are expressed metrically: for example, crown quarto has become 246 × 189mm, and demy quarto 276 × 219mm.

Paper weight

Traditionally, paper was weighed in pounds per ream. A ream of crown bond paper, for example, would weigh 15 lb. There was inevitably confusion with papers of different thicknesses but of similar sizes, so paper everywhere is now assessed in grams per square metre ('gsm'). This grammage is the weight of a square metre of that particular paper. This applies to reels as well as sheets.

Establishing the grain

Experiment with the following tests, until a clear result is obtained.

1. Cut two strips 100 × 12mm at right angles from one corner of a sheet, and mark one to identify its original position. Hold them together by the ends and dampen them with the mouth. One strip will remain upright and the other will collapse in a curve (15A). The grain direction runs the length of the one that is erect.

2. Lay a sheet on the bench; curve over one side until the bend in the paper remains (15B). Measure the distance from the edge to the curve, then bend the other side. If the paper springs back flat, it indicates the fibres are resisting the bending action and that this is not the grain direction.

3. Hold the sheet in one hand by a corner and, beginning from this corner, run the finger and thumb tightly along one edge. Repeat this from the same corner along the other edge. The edge running against the grain will be corrugated, as the fibres are stretched apart. The edge with the grain will be straight or very gently curved.

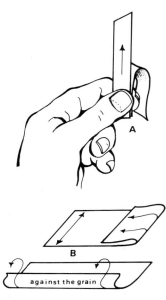

15. Establishing the grain of paper

Once the grain direction has been established, it should be indicated by a pencilled arrow in one corner to avoid errors when cutting. Paper folded with the grain will stay creased without damage. If it is folded against the grain, the fibres will crack and endeavour to straighten out. Any book containing sections folded against the grain will gape.

When moisture in the form of adhesive is applied to paper, it will stretch. The amount of stretch will depend on the type of paper and the water content of the adhesive. Generally paper will stretch eight times as much against the grain as it will with it. This fact must be considered when binding, to control the warping of the boards. (Handmade paper, having no grain direction, will stretch evenly both ways.)

Storage

Paper should be stored in a plans chest, or placed flat between larger sheets of strawboard, to keep out dust and light. A few crystals of Paradichlorobenzene sprinkled in storage areas will prevent depredation by insects.

Adhesives

Adhesives used in bookbinding are paste, animal glues, cold glues, polyvinyl acetate (PVA) and instant glues. Only the first three adhesives, being organic, are recommended for the beginner. Adhesives from organic sources can be dissolved by water and should therefore be used for bindings which may have to be restored in the future. Such adhesives have stood the test of time, but are liable to deterioration in abnormal conditions, such as excess moisture and high temperatures, and to attack by bacteria, fungus and insects.

Paste. Made from starch grain from potato, rice, corn and cassava. It is obtainable prepared in powder form, and is stirred a little at a time into cold water. Further thickening will occur a few minutes after mixing. Only enough should be made for the day's use as it will lose its adhesive properties if kept for longer. The following recipe can be stored in a refrigerator for a number of days.

    100 g. (3½ oz.) plain flour
    1 level tsp. alum
    ½ litre (1 pint) cold water
    2 drops formaldehyde

Blend the flour, alum and a little of the water in a double saucepan until smooth, then gradually add the rest of the water. Heat, stirring constantly, until the mixture thickens. Remove from the heat, place a piece of polythene over the paste to prevent a skin forming, and allow to cool. Stir in the formaldehyde, which acts as a preservative. The cold paste may be thinned by adding water.

21

Paste is a perfect adhesive, as it is absorbed into the pores of the material, making a clean, firm, flexible bond which is therefore less likely to be affected by humidity. Its high water content gives it stretching properties that are used to advantage in various binding operations. Paste is applied by a brushing action (16).

Animal glue (Scotch glue). Made from gelatine extracted from bones, hooves and horns of animals from which the grease has been removed by solvents. It is obtained in cake and pellet form. Flexible glue is animal glue to which glycerine has been added to prevent it from hardening. It may, for example, be applied to the spine of the book which is under tension while in use. A heated glue pot is necessary (8), and for best results hot water is added to the glue until the mixture runs freely from the brush and is the colour of honey. Excess boiling will cause the glue to deteriorate. The water content is much less than paste and on application the glue tends to remain on the surface of the material. This controls stretching and prevents the penetration of the glue through sensitive materials. First stir it with the brush to dissolve the skin on the surface. Wipe and turn the brush on the metal rod across the top of the pot until the sides of the brush are clear. Apply it with a stabbing action (16). Puddles of glue will occur if the brush is overloaded. Wash out brushes at the end of each day's work.

Cold glue. Derived either from casein (milk) or dextrine (starch) it is highly recommended, as it can be used thick for instant adhesion ('grab'), or thin for convenience in positioning the material. Additional qualities are its consistency, cleanliness, lack of waste and odourlessness. It can be dissolved in water, and brushes used for it do not deteriorate as fast as for hot glue. Apply it with a stabbing action, as for animal glue.

Polyvinyl acetate (PVA). A synthetic product derived from oil, which in its liquid state can be thinned with water, but which needs strong solvents when dry. As it cannot be dissolved by water and its lasting qualities are not proven, it should not be used for craft binding. It is, however, convenient for ephemeral work, such as portfolios and boxes. Its advantages are that it comes in a made-up solution, it is consistent in quality and easy to apply. It is, moreover, unaffected by humidity, fungus and insects and is thus a perfect adhesive for tropical countries. Apply it with a stabbing action, as for animal glue. Brushes must be washed out after use.

Instant glue. Many varieties exist, both organic and synthetic, but are both too expensive for general use. Their use is limited to the construction of boxes prior to covering, as their instant 'grab' precludes manipulation while placing the materials.

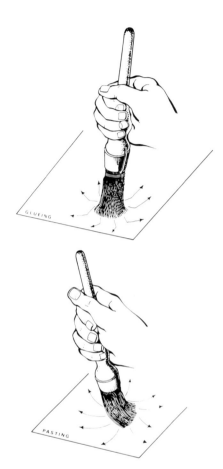

16. Applying glue (above) and paste (below)

22

3
The make-up of a book

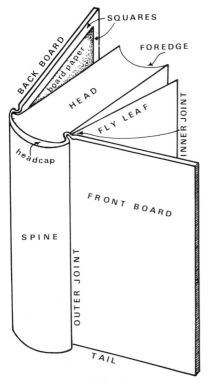

17. Parts of a book

Labels: BACK BOARD, board paper, SQUARES, FOREDGE, HEAD, FLY LEAF, INNER JOINT, headcap, FRONT BOARD, SPINE, OUTER JOINT, TAIL

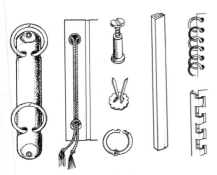

18. Loose-leaf bindings

Books are either made from single leaves or from a number of sheets folded to make sections. The former, when held together by means of spring mechanisms, cord, posts, rivets, rings, bars, spiral wire or plastic combs, are described as 'loose-leaf bindings' (18). The advantages of these so-called temporary bindings are that sheets may be removed, others added and the leaves will open flat. (See also Project 9, Photograph Album, p.79.) However, the inner margins are weakened by the slot or hole perforations. Numbers of single sheets can also be joined by adhesives applied to the binding margin. Called 'unsewn bindings', they are mass produced and have a limited life. Single sheets may be held together by wire or thread stitching which pierces the margin, but these, like adhesive-bound books, have a restricted opening (19).

Books made up of one or more folded sheets ('single-section' or 'multi-section') are sewn through the middle of the section and therefore will open fully. A sheet can be printed with 4, 8, 12, 16 or 32 pages of text, depending on its size, and using both sides of the paper. Sheets of 64 and 128 pages can be economically printed on paper double and four times the standard size (see Paper Sizes, p.19). These are cut into smaller sheets before folding. The order in which these pages are positioned on the sheet is known as the 'imposition'; this can be done in a number of ways, so that when the sheet is printed and folded the page numbers run consecutively. A standard imposition of 16 pages can be arrived at by the following exercise: fold a sheet of paper in half from right to left so that the fold is parallel to the short side ('folio'); fold it again from top to bottom ('quarto'); and a third time from left to right ('octavo'). Number the pages 1 to 16. When the sheet is opened, the imposition will be made clear (20). It will be

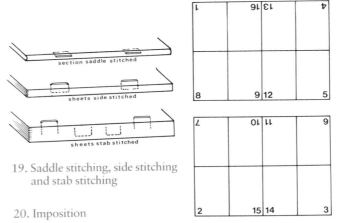

19. Saddle stitching, side stitching and stab stitching

Labels: section saddle stitched, sheets side stitched, sheets stab stitched

20. Imposition

23

observed that the top inner folds have unsightly creases and that the margins are distorted. This is the result of air trapped within the section, and is avoided by slitting the second fold (the 'bolt') more than half way across before making the third fold. Simple machine folding also follows the above procedure, and the bolt is perforated by a toothed cutting disc. The printer will make sure that the grain of the paper will run from the top of the book to the bottom when the sheets are folded. Occasionally printed type may be out of square with the edge of the sheet; the sheet is then folded by lining up the top lines of type ('folding to print') rather than by lining up the edges of the paper ('folding to paper').

Preliminary pages

Traditionally, the first pages of the book are arranged as follows: the first page is sometimes blank but more often has the title (or a shortened version) printed on it, and is called the 'half-title page'. The second leaf may bear an illustration, which is sometimes printed on different paper and 'tipped on' (attached by a thin line of paste along the inner edge of the leaf), or else printed on the reverse side ('verso') of the half-title page. Known as the frontispiece, it faces the 'title page'. This gives the complete title and subtitle, author and publisher, and also, if appropriate, the name of the patron, the date of publication, the volume number, number of illustrations and place of publication. The following pages consist of the 'imprint', or 'copyright', page (which contains copyright information and sometimes acknowledgements and dedication), contents page, and also a list of illustrations, preface, notes, etc., according to the nature of the work. This collection of leaves may be contained in an 8- or 16-page section, although extra leaves may be necessary (see below). The whole is known as the 'preliminary matter' or 'prelims'. In many books the prelims are numbered with roman numerals as they are printed separately, after the rest of the text has been imposed and the page numbers finalized. The first page of the first chapter will then begin on a right-hand page ('recto').

The order of sections

The number of leaves that make up a section can be ascertained by counting the leaves until the sewing thread appears, and then counting this number of leaves until the end of the section is reached. Illustrations printed on different paper must be ignored. On the first page of each section, printed usually in the bottom right-hand corner, is a letter or number called a 'signature'. These signatures run in alphabetical or numerical order and act as an aid to gathering the sections in the correct order for binding. Signature 'A' (or 1) is the prelims (although it is seldom printed) and 'B' (or 2) is the first text section. The letters J, Q and V are sometimes omitted to avoid confusion with I, O and U. The 24th and subsequent sections are signatured 'AA', 'Aa' or 'A1' at the whim of the printer. Should extra leaves be placed into a section, the first page of this inset will be signatured the same as the section, but the letter will be followed by an asterisk.

A further aid to gathering consists of small black rectangles printed on the back fold of each section, in a step sequence (21). Some modern books may not be numbered or signatured, and to avoid misplaced sections the leaves should be numbered in pencil before the book is taken apart for rebinding.

21. Signature marks

Illustrations

Sections are often increased by illustrations and maps printed on different paper (the former being known as 'plates'). They are added in the following ways (22):

A. As single plates tipped on or within a section. These have the advantage of being close to their reference in the text, but the attachment is weak and the next leaf has a restricted opening. On rebinding, these plates should be removed and hinge guarded in their original position (28).

B. As 4-page sections folded around or within the text sections and sewn in.

C. As complete sections distributed evenly throughout the book.

D. As complete sections placed all together, usually at the end of the book. This method is common to art books. The text is usually printed on soft paper and the illustrations on hard, art paper, which makes an ill-balanced book.

Folded diagrams and maps, rarely secured in mass-produced books, soon tear and detach from the binding. The craft binder should remove them when the sections are separated and replace them with a new false section strengthened with a cloth hinge during the binding process (23). When the book has been bound, the false section is cut away and replaced with the folded work securely glued to the cloth hinge.

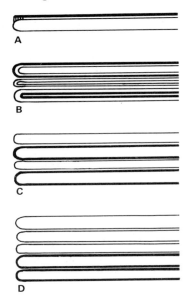

22. Arrangement of plates (shown by thick lines)

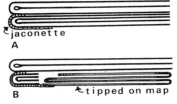

23. Hinge guarding a folded map. The false section is shown in A; in B it is cut away and the map tipped onto the hinge in its place

4
Design and decoration

The design of a binding lies primarily in its construction. The strength incorporated into the binding and the quality of the materials should be the first concern of the beginner: the addition of coloured leathers as decoration, fancy papers and gold tooling will be useless if the book is not made strong enough to last. Bindings are, however, enhanced by harmonious colours, textured materials and gold titles.

The binding is given extra protection by being covered with leather or cloth all over or down the spine and over the corners (24). The quarter and half styles of covering are economical in materials but often involve more work. These combinations of leather and cloth or of cloth and paper can be very attractive provided that their proportion is correct. As a general rule, the width of cloth or leather on the sides is one quarter of the width of the book, and the diagonal of the corner pieces (104) should also be one quarter of the width of the book. The foredge strip should be a little less than a quarter.

24. Covering styles: quarter, half with corners, half with foredge strip, whole

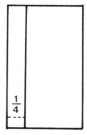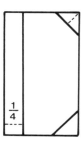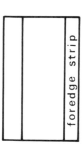

A study of the colour circle will be of help in choosing harmonious colours for binding materials (25). The primary colours are yellow, red and blue. The secondary colours (orange, violet and green) are made by mixing two primaries in equal proportions. Colours mixed in unequal proportions produce an infinitesimal range of tertiary colours. Warm colours are in the range yellow-orange-red, and cold colours in the range green-blue-violet. Harmonious colours are adjacent, and discordant colours are opposite, in the colour circle. A knowledge of the book's content is important for choosing a colour for the cover, for a judicious choice can help to express its character. It would be both odd and tasteless to use discordant colours on a book of romantic poetry, for example. Discords may be used on books of a violent nature to express a feeling of chaos and unease, but on the whole harmonious colours are more acceptable, as books have a part in our homes and lives.

25. Colour circle

Decorated papers

Bindings of no particular value may be covered attractively with paper decorated in a simple way. Traditionally, papers were always decorated by the bookbinder himself, and the student should start with the following exercises before tackling the projects, to gain an appreciation of design and colour harmonies; the creation of such papers will be found a highly satisfying task in itself, and will also give confidence in the use of materials.

Paste graining

This is an old method which produces pleasant, naive patterns of infinite variety.

Assemble the following materials:

> paste (thin consistency; see recipe on p.21)
> good quality water-soluble paint (e.g. gouache)
> well-sized white cartridge drawing paper
> glue brush
> waste paper

Mix the paste with the paint, using various colours in unequal proportions to obtain subtle tones. When brushed onto the paper, the colours should almost obliterate the surface. Anything then scraped, pulled or pressed across this surface while it is wet will cause a mark. The paste should be thin, the colour intense and the pattern completed before the paste soaks into the surface. Experiment initially with the following methods:

1. Using a glue brush, rapidly cover the surface of the paper with a thick layer of coloured paste. Spread the finger tips and, with an irregular and haphazard circular movement, rub them over the surface. Place the paper on a sheet of waste paper to dry.

2. Screw up a handful of waste paper and dab this regularly over the wet surface. Dry as before.

3. Brush the paste onto the paper and crumple the sheet into a ball with the wet surface inside. Open it out carefully and dry as before.

4. Brush on the paste and then, starting from one corner, twist the glue brush on the surface in a circular movement. Repeat this regularly and evenly across and down the sheet. Dry as before.

5. Brush on the paste. Fold the paper with the wet side inside and slide the two halves apart. Dry as before.

Controlled and formal patterns can also be designed using decorator's combs (26). Infinite patterning can be achieved using these combs, or indeed any object that will make a mark. Variations include the use of coloured paper and combing an additional pattern onto an

26. Decorator's combs

already combed and dried sheet. These paste-grained papers are permanent, as the colour is 'fixed' by the paste.

Water marbling

Oil colour floating on glue water can be transferred onto paper to create random patterns. As no two can be the same, paper large enough to cover both sides of the binding must be used.

Assemble the following materials:

    photographer's dish
    glue (hot or cold)
    7 wide-necked jars
    artists' tube oil colours or printing ink
    white spirit
    7 sprinkle brushes (made by gathering small bunches of bristles from a garden broom and tying them tightly together at one end)
    paper (good quality cartridge)
    waste paper

Pour warm water into the dish to a depth of 25mm and add glue until the water goes a light brown. (This slightly viscous liquid stops the oil colours on the surface from moving about too much and mixing together.) Mix white spirit with a little of each colour in the jars, to a thin consistency. (The popular colours are the three primaries, the secondaries and black. Mix other colours in separate containers if required.) Using a separate brush for each colour, dip the tip of the brush into the colour and flick it over the bath until the surface is generously covered with spots of colour. Repeat with two or more colours, and it will be found that they will remain separate. Hold a sheet of paper by opposite edges to form a curved surface and lower it, centre first, onto the bath. Care should be taken not to trap any air under the paper. Lift off the sheet, drain the surplus water from it and place it on waste paper to dry. Repeat with another sheet of paper. After a few attempts the bath will improve, as the surface will be covered with a thin neutral-coloured film that acts as a background to other patterns. (It can, however, be cleaned by laying a sheet of newspaper across the surface to absorb excess colours.) To add interest, lay the colours as usual but swirl the surface with a thin stick in a rhythmic, controlled movement to achieve a 'marbling' result.

Professional marbling is beyond the range of this book, as more equipment and a special-size bath is required. The student should enquire at schools of bookbinding (see list on p.93) into the Carragheen Moss method for interest and advancement.

Other methods of decorating paper

These are too numerous to explain in detail here, but common ones include linocuts, stick and potato prints, stencils and patterns made by calligraphic pens. Students are advised to experiment with these as well, as they have individual characteristics appropriate to books. (Whichever method is used, it is important to ensure that patterns made with vertical motifs should have these running *with* the grain of the paper; see p.18.)

I would urge the beginner to create his or her own decorated papers, for personal satisfaction, rather than resorting to bought ones.

Other methods of decoration

Books can be decorated in several ways: a cloth case, for example, can be embossed by cutting out shapes from cardboard and, before the endpapers are pasted down, placing them on the cover and pressing them in the nipping press under considerable pressure for ten seconds. Alternatively, covers could be decorated with large linocuts or free ink drawings illustrating the contents of the book. Cloth, cut out and stuck onto cases in an imaginative way, would be a good introduction to the use of onlayed leather work on advanced bindings (see *The Thames and Hudson Manual of Bookbinding*, pp.206-10).

In all design work, colour sketches should be made, to size, to plan proportion, layout and colour harmony.

Working procedures

5 Endpapers

The endpapers are part of the binding construction and not of the text. There are many types of endpaper, but a basic one consists of a folded sheet of paper, one half of which, known as the board paper, is stuck to the inside of the book cover, front and back, to counteract the pull or warp caused by the covering material, and the other, known as the fly leaf or free leaf, remains unattached, and protects the first or last leaf of the text.

Strong, good quality papers are used for endpapers, e.g. drawing cartridge and Abbey Mill printing paper. Mould-made Italian, Swedish and French Ingres papers are recommended for high quality work. The pH value of the paper (see p.13) should be around neutral; hence mechanical wood pulp papers, which are acidic, are not used. Handmade paper is suitable for endpapers on certain bindings, but problems arise in adhesion and stretching, and it should only be used in advanced work.

The colour of the endpapers should harmonize with the covering cloth, and fly leaves can be of off-white paper toning with the text paper. Pure white fly leaves are inappropriate next to grey or yellowish text paper.

Preparing the endpapers

First ensure that the grain direction of the paper runs from head to tail, even if this means cutting to waste.

Cut the endpapers 12mm larger than the text paper, as it is difficult to stick sheets of the same size together accurately. It is simple to cut them to size when made. Use paste rather than glue for making up the endpapers, as it is less affected by humidity, allows a longer working time, is clean in use and dries away to make a flexible yet efficient bond. (When making the more complex endpapers, such as the common made endpaper, 27D, where the whole leaf has to be pasted, paste the thicker paper if more than one type is used, to avoid excessive stretching.)

Place the folded sheet on a large piece of waste paper and paste it from the middle outwards (16), with little paste on the brush, to avoid 'layering' of the adhesive. Continue until the crinkles disappear and the paper lies flat, when it will be fully stretched. Hairs from the brush or other matter can be removed with a finger. Hold the sheet by its edges and transfer to clean waste. Place the other unpasted, folded sheet to line up both folded edges. Without hesitation or examination place both between clean pressing boards and nip in the press. Take out after five seconds and check for cleanliness and excess paste. If unmarked and stuck firmly, place between boards under a heavy weight to dry.

Never hang endpapers on string lines to dry, as they may cockle. Always plan the making of endpapers so that they will be dry when one marks up for sewing.

Types of endpaper

The better the quality of the binding, the more complicated its endpapers. The seven styles illustrated are sufficient for the work described in the projects, and some may be used as variants.

KEY

Coloured paper	———
White paper	——
Cloth	═══
Waste sheet	- - - - -
Position of sewing thread	•
Paste	/////////////
Waste sheet	W
Fly leaves	F
Board paper	B
Stiff leaf	SL
First section	S

27A. Simple 4-page 'tipped on' endpaper. Used for cased work in mass-produced hardback bindings. It consists of one folded sheet placed at the front and back of the book. It protects the text pages and counteracts the warp (see above), but adds little strength to the binding. It is attached to the first and last sections by a 5mm layer of paste ('tipped on') along the back folds, and allowed to dry under a weight. Care should be taken while forwarding, as the board paper is vulnerable to damage.

27B. A variation on the 4-page endpaper, but considerably stronger; ideal for multi-section pamphlets that are to be well used. The board paper is reinforced by a 50mm strip of jaconette which is stuck down under the board paper to strengthen the board hinge. This jaconette flange is pasted round the first section to a width of 5mm and sewn through with it. It is recommended that this endpaper be used as a variation for the multi-section case binding in Project 5.

27C. Simple endpaper of two folded, coloured papers wrapped around a single-section pamphlet and sewn in with the text. Additional white folds can be added as further fly leaves. It is used for ephemeral pamphlet work.

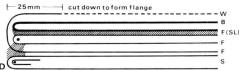

27D. Common made endpaper. The most versatile endpaper for all good quality work. The term 'made' indicates that two or more sheets of paper or board are stuck together. (This endpaper originated at the beginning of the nineteenth century when flimsy marbled paper was used for endpapers, which bore the stains of

31

the marbling process on the back. It therefore required lining with white paper. This endpaper is still used for marbled paper today, and for plain coloured paper.) The strengthened leaf of double thickness is known as a 'stiff leaf'. Whether this leaf adds to the protection of the text is arguable, but it is certainly clumsy in small books. The endpaper is made up of two folded sheets of white paper and one folded sheet of coloured for each end of the book. It has two white fly leaves and a stiff leaf which is coloured on one side, white on the other. The endpapers are sewn in with the sections and are additionally secured by being tipped onto the first and last sections (44). For Project 5, the endpapers illustrated in 27B and 27E can be used as variations.

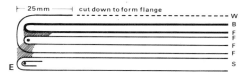

27E. *A variation on the common made endpaper*, the only difference being that the coloured and white papers are not pasted together to form the stiff leaf. An appealing arrangement is to use Ingres paper of different tones of the same colour, e.g. a dark blue board paper, and a light blue for the fly leaf (or 'white'). This may be used as a variant in case work.

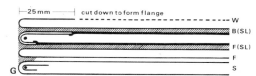

27F. *Hidden cloth-jointed endpaper*. Used for books which will be put to considerable use, and whose appearance is important, e.g. music bindings. The addition of a jaconette joint to the endpapers adds to the strength of the binding at the hinges. The cloth may be put into the split board of a library-style binding (see Project 6) or between the board and the board paper (see Project 7).

27G. *Exposed cloth-jointed endpaper*. Used for bindings which are to be subjected to hard wear but for which elegance is a secondary factor. So called because the reinforcing cloth is exposed and gives extra strength to the joint. Books such as lending-library and reference books need bookcloth joints 25mm wide for small volumes, and thicker cloth, up to 45mm wide, for larger ones. If the colours of cloth, endpapers and covering are planned harmoniously the result can be very attractive. (Sewing this endpaper differs from the others in that the thread runs continuously along the fold, as in 35H.)

6 Repairs

As in most binding operations, it is essential to ensure that the grain direction of text and repair papers are the same. A collection of various types of paper is essential in order that satisfactory repairs can be made.

Repairing the back folds

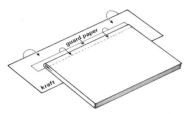

28. Repairing the back fold and hinge guarding

For each fold to be repaired, cut a strip ('guard') of bond paper 12mm by 25mm longer than the section. Apply paste to the guard, leaving a fingerhold dry at one end, and lay it on a piece of kraft paper, paste side up. Line up the head of the section to the top of the guard and half way across it (28). Pull the kraft around the section, fold it and rub it down with a folder. Snip off the excess guard at the tail.

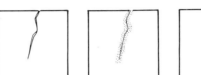

29A

Tears

If necessary, separate the four-page fold from the section. Paste either side of the tear for 3mm and position the two sides together with a needle, making sure that no type is obliterated. Select a tissue paper such as lens or Japanese tissue to tone with the text, place it over the tear and rub it down with a folder (29A). Repeat the process on the other side and leave to dry, interleaved with waxed paper. Tear off the excess tissue against the pasted area, then smooth it down with a folder. Replace the fold in its original position within the section.

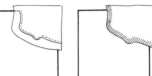

29B

Missing parts

Separate the four-page fold from the section if necessary. Proceed with either of the following two methods.

The first method makes a satisfactory repair but may involve a loss of printed matter. Choose a replacement paper matching in substance and tone and position it under the leaf. Mark the outline of the missing area with the head of a needle as in 29B. Tear the piece of replacement paper 3mm larger than the missing portion and pare both the edge and the underside of the leaf for 3mm with a scalpel. Thinly paste the edges of the hole and the replacement paper and marry them together, rubbing them down with a folder. When dry, trim off the excess.

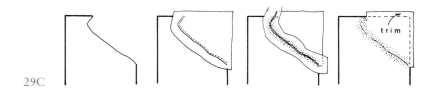

29C

When it is important not to lose any printed matter, use the second method. Position the replacement paper as before, and trace the outline with the point of a needle (29C). Tease away the fibres until it fits exactly. Position the two, paste both edges for 3mm and lay on tissue and rub down. Repeat on the other side and leave to dry. Tear off excess as before, and smooth down with a folder. Replace the repaired fold in its original position within the section.

Dirty marks

Remove these with an eraser, starting with a soft one, and then a harder one if necessary.

Dog-eared corners

These should be dampened, straightened and pressed flat under a weight until dry.

After any repairs, it is important to let the sections dry thoroughly before the book is pressed.

7
Sewing techniques

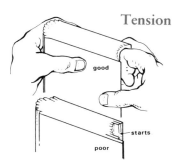

30. Pushing in the foredge to test for even sewing

Tension

Even-tensioned sewing will greatly facilitate all subsequent binding operations. Sewing, once started, should be completed without interruption, as any break in concentration and the rhythmic movement of the needle will change the tension of the thread. If one or two sections are sewn too tight or too loose, the spine will be uneven and 'starts' will appear at the foredge. Illustration 30 shows a test for evenness. It is not necessary to pull thread very tight, as this puts the fibres under strain and there will be difficulty in shaping the spine.

Swell

Besides holding the sections together, the thread must provide a 'swell' in the back folds so that backing can be accomplished (43). Too little swell causes the spine of the book to collapse and leads to the breakdown of the sewing. Too much swell makes backing extremely difficult: it restricts the opening and imposes a strain on the spine, which again causes a breakdown. The aim is to shape the spine into a third of a circle (43A-C). For every book it is advisable to sew the first five sections 'all along' (see below), with thread selected as below. Now estimate the swell (or lack of it) by feel. Dividing the unsewn number of sections by five will give a reasonable estimate of the likely swell.

Thread

Select the thread carefully, according to the following criteria, as there is no universal thread for sewing, and every book should be assessed differently.

Type of paper. A thick thread should be used for soft, unsized paper as a thin one will sink into the sections, with no resulting swell. On the other hand, handmade and hard art paper will resist the thread, and excess swell may occur; a thinner thread should therefore be chosen.

Number of sections. The greater the number of sections the greater the swell. If necessary, swell can be reduced by using thinner thread or by beating the thread into the paper with a loaded stick (a stick weighted at one end) after every three sections. Alternatively, sew the first four and the last four sections with a medium thread, to ensure strong joints, and use a thinner thread for the remainder.

Thickness of the sections. Thick sections are sewn with little difficulty, but use a thick thread to provide enough swell. Numerous thin sections are a problem, and one may need to sew the first six sections and the last six 'all along' (the thread running through each section in turn; see below) to make sound shoulders while the rest are sewn 'two up' (through two sections; see below) to reduce the swell. Should this be necessary, it is imperative that two extra tapes are used on the frame to secure the sections.

Binding style. This will also affect the choice of thread. In volumes such as music bindings, small Bibles and account books, for example, which are rounded but not backed (see p.43), excess swell is justified to retain the shape of the spine.

Mixed papers. If a book is made up of sections of different papers (for example art books, which are often printed on soft paper which comprises part of the book, while the illustrations are on hard, glossy art paper), a thicker thread must be used for the text and a thinner for the remainder to balance the swell and create a symmetrical binding.

Repairs. If a section is repaired or strengthened, there will be extra thicknesses of paper in the back fold. Many repairs can cause an excess swell even before sewing.

35

Use a very thin thread or resort to the 'two up' method (35A). Alternatively, reduce the swell by using thinner repair paper, or by pressing or beating the folds of the sections with a hammer.

Joining the thread

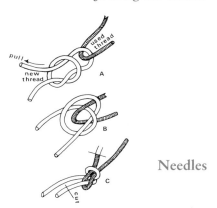

Lengths of thread should not be too long, as they tend to become twisted and knotted, making sewing laborious and frustrating. Join lengths of thread with a weaver's knot, as in 31. This has the following advantages: it will not pull free; two threads of unequal thickness can be joined securely; the knot can be made exactly where required; and one thread can be as short as 6mm. Knots are made on the outside of the sections for convenience, but are pulled inside as sewing progresses.

Needles

Use strong, large-eyed needles, as a number of sheets have to be pierced at once. Fix them to the thread as in 32.

31. Weaver's knot

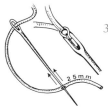

32. Fixing the thread to the needle

Marking up for sewing

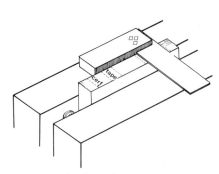

'Knock up' the sections (i.e. tap the head and spine on the bench until the sections are aligned) and screw them in a finishing press. Use a carpenter's square to check that the head is at right angles and that all the sections are level (33). Cut tapes as required for the binding concerned and arrange them on the back of the sections so that the distance between each tape, and at the head and tail, are the same. Then move all the tapes 3mm nearer the head (optical centering). Make pencil marks on the sections, alongside the edges of the tapes, and make two further marks 15mm from head and tail for the cerfs (channels cut in the sections to accommodate the knots). Then, using a carpenter's square, emphasize the lines alongside the tapes, to facilitate placing the needle. Pinch the sections together and saw in the cerfs with a tenon saw. The cut should be no more than the depth of the teeth of the saw. Endpapers should not be cut, but the cerf marked with a pencil. Remove the sections from the press.

33. Checking that the sections are level

36

How to sew   Set up the sewing frame as in 5. Place a pressing board on the frame, to make it easier to sew the first section. Place the first or last section on the frame, and lay all the others aside on the bench, with the next section to be sewn at the top of the pile. Sit at either end, with the frame at an angle, depending on whether you are left- or right-handed, so that you can reach the inside of the section with one hand and the outside with the other. Check that the signatures and page numbers are correct. Knock up the section and sew only through the centre fold. Sew the book according to one of the following methods, as stipulated in the appropriate project.

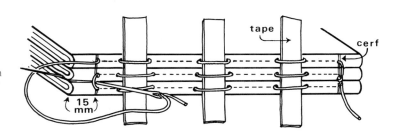

34. All along sewing, showing how to make the kettle stitch

'All along' sewing   Sew the first section, which is usually the endpaper, as follows. Insert the needle into the cerf or pencil mark from the outside. Sew along the section, around the tapes, and pull the needle out through the cerf at the other end. Now pull the thread through the section, in the direction of sewing in order to avoid tearing the paper, leaving 50mm at the beginning.

Place the second section on top of the first and continue by inserting the needle through its cerf and sew as before, until the end is reached. Line up the two sections at the head, pull both ends of the thread tightly, and tie them together with a reef knot (square knot), so that it sinks into the cerf.

Place the third section on top of the first two and insert the needle into the cerf as before, and sew the section until the thread comes out of the cerf. Now pass the needle under the previous section, as in 34, so that the point protrudes at the side of the book. Hook a loop of the thread over the needle, and pull the needle through so that the thread tightens and the knot is made into the cerf. This is a 'kettle stitch', and must not protrude from the cerf.

Continue sewing the next sections in the same way, making a kettle stitch at the end of each section to join it to the last. At the end of the last section, make two kettle stitches on top of each other and cut the thread, leaving 25mm to be glued onto the spine.

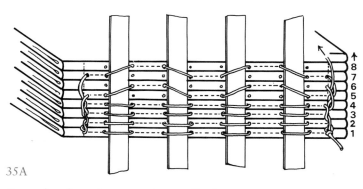

35A

Sewing 'two up'

Sew the first four sections all along, to ensure strong shoulders at the joint. Place the fifth section in position and push the needle into its cerf and out at the first tape. Position the sixth section and push the needle into this section so the thread is diagonally across the first tape. Continue along the sixth section until the needle is pushed out at the second tape, then pass the thread diagonally into the fifth section. Sew the fifth section until the next tape; go into the sixth section and continue until the cerf is reached, depending on the number of tapes. Make the kettle stitch (see above) at the fourth section, then push the needle into the cerf at the seventh section. Sew the seventh and eighth sections as the previous two. Continue in this way, making kettle stitches on both sides, until the last four sections, which should be sewn all along to give balance to the spine. (A thin strip of card placed in the centre of the section not being sewn at the time will facilitate finding its middle.)

Other sewing techniques

All the other techniques used in the projects are illustrated and described below.

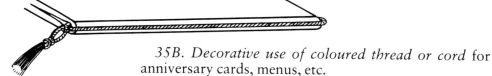

35B. Decorative use of coloured thread or cord for anniversary cards, menus, etc.

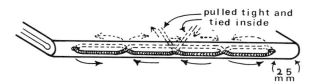

35C. Single-section pamphlet sewing, with 3, 5, 7 or more holes depending on the length of the book and the number of leaves to the section. Swell is obviously not a consideration, but it is essential that the two ends of the thread are pulled tight on either side of the long middle thread and tied with a reef knot (square knot).

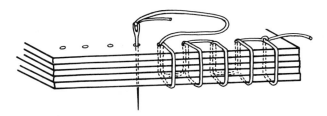

35D. Blanket stitching, or side stitching, for numbers of single sheets. Opening is restricted.

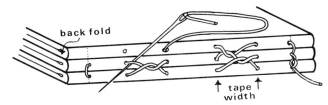

35E. 'French sewing' (without tape). This method is used for Bibles, limp bindings and most mass-produced cased work for cheapness, but is not recommended for craft work where strength is the first consideration. The sections are marked up as for tape sewing, and the same sewing technique used as for 'all along' (see above), except that the thread is linked on the outside to the previous section as illustrated here.

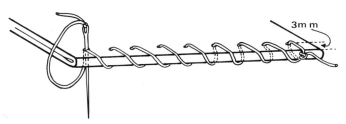

35F. Overcasting the first and last sections of text with very thin thread to strengthen the beginning and end of a book in the library style. Both ends of the thread are tied with a knot. Since these sections, with the endpapers, are shaped permanently by the backing (80B), overcasting does not restrict movement.

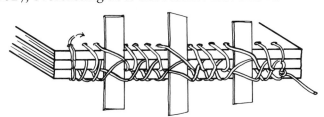

35G. Overcasting groups of single leaves onto each other around tapes, with the cerf omitted. Mark up with tapes as before. Having secured the thread in the first hole with a knot, overcast the first collection of about eight single sheets (depending on the paper thickness)

through their margins around the tape (bottom section). Go around the last stitch twice. Continue the thread into the second section, which is overcast through the first, and a knot made at the end. The third group is overcast through the second, and so on. A restricted opening is inevitable.

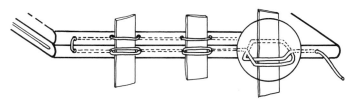

35H. Double sewing the exposed cloth-jointed endpaper in the library style, with the second and subsequent sections sewn all along (see above) with continuous thread.

8 Edge trimming

The aim of edge trimming is to make the edges even, to facilitate the turning of the pages. It will also help to keep the dust out. Although deckle-edged paper (see p. 17) is often left uncut as it is considered attractive, this broken edge remains a dust trap. (Cutting the head is unavoidable, in order to free the pages.)

Some early books have been disfigured and made almost valueless by indiscriminate edge trimming. The proportion of text to margin in old and precious books must be preserved, and so the edges of these should never be trimmed. Throughout this book cutting is recommended as a means of developing skills in the use of equipment, and is to be practised on books of little value.

The following general rules apply:

1. The minimum trim should be 1mm less than the smallest page, and the maximum trim 3mm.

2. The guide lines for cutting must be accurate and the work correctly positioned in the press.

3. Knives and blades must be very sharp.

4. An intense and even pressure should be maintained on the book edge in the cutting press.

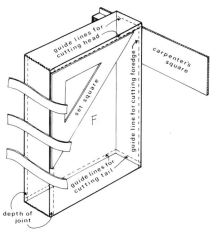

36. Guide lines for cutting head, foredge and tail

Preparing the press and marking up for cutting

Open the lying press, cutting side uppermost, a little wider than the thickness of the book. Have ready two cutting boards and millboards and sharpen the plough blade (see p.12). Mark up the book for cutting, with guide lines on the front for cutting the head and foredge and on the back for cutting the tail (36). Continue these lines across the sections on the foredge. (The foredge is cut before the book is rounded and backed, and the head and tail afterwards. Swell caused by the sewing thread is obviated by the rounded spine. Should there be a slight deviation from the square after backing, it can be corrected by careful trimming. See Chapter 9, where instructions for marking the guide line for the joint are also given.)

Method 1
(with cutting boards)

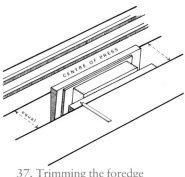

37. Trimming the foredge
(Method 1)

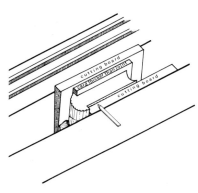

38. Trimming the head and tail
(Method 1)

Place a cutting board on top of the lying press, face it with a piece of millboard and position the book on it so that the cutting line of the foredge is below the top of the board. Lay a second cutting board on top, flush with the guide line. Slide book, millboard and both cutting boards towards the edge of the press. Pick them up in one hand and lower them into the centre of the press, foredge uppermost, until they hold. Standing at one end of the press, give both screws a slight turn to open it. This allows book and boards to be pushed lower into the press without disturbing their positions. Repeat this turning and pushing movement until the board on the guide line is level with the surface of the press (37). It is extremely important that the guide line is accurately positioned at this stage, otherwise the whole book will be out of square. As the plough blade must run flat on top of the cutting board, some slight adjustment of the blade in the plough may be necessary. The student should practise this positioning to gain skill and confidence before cutting. It is better to attempt to place the book in the press a number of times rather than risk cutting out of square.

Now tighten the press: the pressure will be greatest at the widest part of the wedge, at the cutting point. Place the plough in the runners, clear of the book, as in 37. Make two or three experimental movements with the plough in this position, as follows. Bear down on it, push it firmly along the length of the book edge, along the cutting board, but clear of the edge to be cut. Return the plough without lifting it; turn the screw forward a fraction to advance the blade and thrust forward again. Continue this process until the edges begin to be trimmed. A rhythmic movement of thrust, back, turn; thrust, back, turn will ensure even cutting. No cut is made on the return movement, and excessive turning of the screw will force the blade through too many sheets, resulting in a torn and broken edge. Cut the last few leaves by running the blade into the protecting millboard.

Illustration 38 shows how to set up the press for cutting the head and tail. Ensure that the book is positioned correctly, and make a few preliminary cutting movements as before. Begin by cutting through the joint. It is even more important to cut only on the forward stroke, away from the spine and to cut only one

41

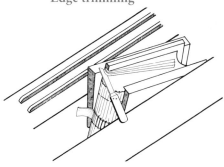

or two sheets at a time. (Cutting on the return movement with the blade over-advanced will break off the unsupported back folds of the sections.) Cut the last leaves against the millboard as before, and cut the remaining joint by loosening the press, raising the book and slicing against the millboard with a sharp knife (39).

39. Trimming the joint

Method 2
(without cutting boards)

The beginner may find this simpler, as it is easier to position the book into the press without the weight of the boards. It does, however, have several disadvantages, viz.:

1. Heavy books cannot be well controlled without the cutting boards.

2. Pressure is not so intense at the cutting point, as it is distributed by the flat boards over the sides of the book. A poor cut may result, especially with pulpy papers. In addition, any embossed illustrations or decorative letters will be flattened by the pressure.

3. Any folded diagrams and photographs inset within the book mean that there is less pressure at the cutting line, which may result in torn edges.

4. If the book or millboard is less than the depth of the cheeks of the press, the swell will be crushed in the press when cutting the foredge.

5. If the edges of the millboard are not bevelled as they should be (40), they will be pressed into the sections, creating unsightly marks.

Set up the press with the book and millboard as in 40, and cut the foredge as in Method 1. For books that are rounded and backed, cut the head and tail as in 41, and for those that are flat backed as in 73.

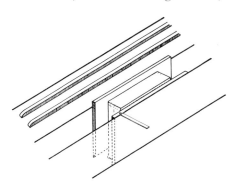

40. Trimming the foredge
(Method 2)

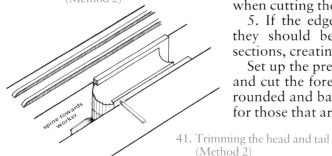

spine towards worker

41. Trimming the head and tail
(Method 2)

Colouring the edge

Although the newly cut edge is attractive, it is very vulnerable to fingermarks. To avoid this, the edge can be coloured or sprinkled with dye. Place the book between pressing boards, with a heavy weight on top. Shield boards and bench with waste paper. Mix watercolour or water dye to harmonize with the colour of the endpapers and subsequent covering materials. To colour the edge, prepare a pad of cotton wool a little wider than the thickness of the book. Dip the pad into the dye and first dab it onto some waste paper to distribute the liquid. Then, with an even pressure, wipe the pad quickly across the edge, endeavouring to cover the area completely at one stroke. For a dark tone, it is best to apply several washes, allowing each to dry before the next.

42. Mouth spray

Sprinkling or 'spotting' is achieved by dipping a toothbrush in the dye and rubbing the bristles towards you on a comb directed at the edge. Alternatively, a mouth spray for fixing charcoal drawings can be used (42). Practise first on a sheet of white paper to determine the size and density of the dots. The use of two colours applied separately can give an attractive result. Spirit dye should be avoided, since the spirit penetrates the edges of the paper and gives unsightly stains.

9
Rounding and backing

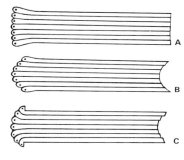

43. The three stages of rounding and backing: A, sewn, with swell; B, rounded; C, rounded and backed

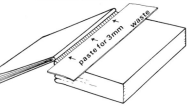

44. Tipping on the first and last sections

These two operations are considered as one continuous process; rounding is the initial curving of the spine (43B) in preparation for backing, which is the creation of joints to support the spine (43C). A backed book therefore is always rounded first.

Backing is an essential contribution to the durability of a book. The sections of a flat-backed book standing on a shelf are suspended between the covers, and are held in place by tape, mull and endpapers. In time, the thread breaks down, the linings loosen, the spine becomes concave, the endpapers pull away and the binding collapses. The flat-backed book opens well but is intended only as a temporary binding. The 'backed' book, on the other hand, although it has a restricted opening, has a considerably longer life.

The book to be backed must first be sewn so that the thread provides sufficient swell to enable the spine to be shaped to a third of a circle with joints (43C). All sections, starting from the centre, are bent over each other at a progressively sharper angle, until the last forms a right angle at the joint. As each section supports the next, there is no strain on the sewing thread, and the lengths of both joints are supported by the upright boards. The effect of gravity is thus reduced. Headbands and headcaps (17) support the spine, and the book stands firmly on the shelf.

Working procedure

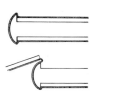

45. Depth of the joint in a case binding

Mark the book up for cutting all three edges, as on p.40. Tip on the endpapers and first and last sections with paste for 3mm along the joint, as they are likely to move out of position as work proceeds (44). Mark the depth of the joint on the endpapers by drawing lines parallel to the spine edge, and the same distance from it as the thickness of the board (which is determined by the weight of the book). This does not apply to case bindings, where the joint should be half as thick again as the board, to allow for the fact that the covering cloth will not fold to a sharp angle at the hinge (45).

Work will proceed more efficiently if tools are laid out before use. These are:

a pair of cutting boards
strips of card for trimming the foredge
a pair of backing boards (10B)
hammer
glue
paste

Prepare the lying press as follows: sharpen the plough blade, fix it in the plough and place this between the runners on the press. Put the sewn sections on the edge of the bench and apply thin glue to the spine and run it between the sections. The student should work quickly and efficiently, as the operations of cutting the foredge, rounding and backing should be completed before this glue has dried. Sections hardened with glue cannot be shaped with a hammer without damage. (Should there be unavoidable delay in the work, paste rubbed on the spine will soften the glue and keep it moist.) Now pick up the book by one edge and 'knock up' to flatten the spine and square up the head (46). Cut the foredge, as in 37. Turn the press over to the backing side.

Immediately after cutting, the book is rounded; this process should take less than a minute. The hand is spread across the book, the thumb pushes the foredge while the fingers pull back the sections. A tapping, wiping action of the backing hammer along the top of the spine will shape half the book into an approximate quarter of a circle (47). Hold the book firmly to prevent the sections from returning to their flat position. Turn the book over and repeat the process. The spine will form a round shape with the foredge becoming correspondingly concave. The book must be square and symmetrically rounded.

Commence backing before the spine is dry. Place the sections on top of the press, retaining the rounded spine. Position the backing boards to the pencilled guide lines at the joint, underneath the tapes. Pick up book and boards firmly in the centre with the fingertips, check for symmetry and push them into the centre of the partly opened press until they hold without slipping. Neither boards nor book should move out of position because of the wedge-shaped boards. Ensure that the cheeks of the press are exactly parallel. Ease open both ends of the press by a fraction of a turn, and, by pressing both book and boards with spread fingers and increasing the opening of the press, level the backing boards with the top of the press. Tighten the screws considerably with the press pin and check alignment with a carpenter's square (48). Any deviation from symmetry is unacceptable, and it may take several attempts to achieve the required result.

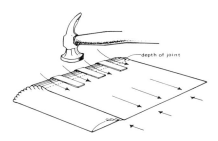

46. Knocking up

47. Rounding: the action of the backing hammer

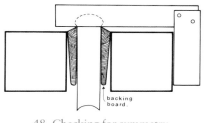

48. Checking for symmetry before backing

44

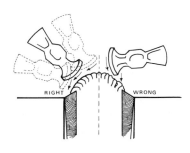

49. Backing: the action of the backing hammer

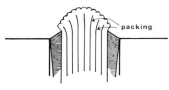

50. Allowing for excess swell by packing

Hold the backing hammer parallel to the plane of the curve and with regular, rhythmic, glancing blows push the sections in neat order, leaving the middle section untouched while the others progressively flatten to the boards. Misdirected blows will crush the sections and the spine will be misshapen (49). The outermost sections should be flattened flush to the bevelled surface of the backing board, using the side of the hammer or its claw. (The hammer is designed for its purpose, the head being dome shaped so that only indirect blows can be given. The axe, or claw part, can also be used and it does not matter how the hammer is handled if the result is satisfactory, although one should avoid making grooves in the spine with the claw. The backing board is bevelled at an obtuse angle so that when pressure is relieved, the sections widen out, pushing the joints back to a right angle.) Remove the book from the press, and cut the head and tail as in 38.

An excess of swell may build up in spite of efforts to control it, causing the backing boards to slip from their positions in the press. In order to avoid this, the book can be packed with strips of thick paper 75 mm wide by the length of the book, their number being dependent on the swell. These are placed evenly throughout the sections up to the guide lines of the joint at the back folds. They bulk out the sections at the joint position and allow backing to continue without too much difficulty (50).

10 Tight and hollow backs

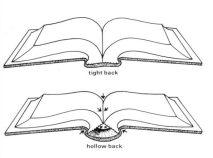

51. Tight and hollow backs, showing the areas of strain in the latter

Books bound in leather are structurally stronger and more durable if the covering is attached directly to the backs of the sections or indirectly to their linings (80). The resulting 'tight back' gives additional support to the sections when standing on the shelf. The spine is flat or slightly concave when the book is opened, which causes a small loss of the inner margin. The covering of a 'hollow-backed' book, on the other hand, is stuck to a paper tube (a 'hollow') attached to the backs of the sections. When in use, the spine retains its round shape, and the sections are 'thrown up', making a good opening. There is, however, a strain on the sewing, linings and joints (51).

Despite the advantages of tight backs, not all books should be so bound: sometimes permanence has to give way to utility. Adjustments must be made for the substance of the paper, the limitations of the covering material, and the use and cost of the binding. A large sheet of thick paper held by its edge will 'fall down' because of its weight, but the same paper postcard size will be inflexible and remain upright. Books of small

45

size but of thick paper are given hollow backs for ease of opening. On the other hand, sections of thin paper fall flat readily and should have tight backs. Books bound in vellum or hard buckram are given hollow backs, as these materials are not flexible enough to move as a tight back. Visitors' books, even if covered with leather, are invariably given a hollow back, so that the leaves will open flat and entries are not restricted. Similarly with lectern Bibles: the text must open well into the inner margins and the leaves lie flat. (Moreover, neither of these types of books are intended to stand upright unsupported.) Thin books have tight backs, as the movement in the spines is so slight as to make a hollow back unnecessary.

Hollow backs are favoured by commercial binders as less work is involved in lining the spines and the firm paper tube provides a smooth base for intricate gold tooling. The spines of cloth-cased bindings are reinforced with a strip of thick paper called a 'stiffener'. Although hollow backs are unavoidable on certain bindings, tight backs should be used for books in permanent use, and for those which are to be preserved and treasured.

Working procedure for hollows

Set the book in a finishing press and cut a strip of good quality kraft paper four times the width of the spine and a little over its length. Apply glue to the spine, line up one edge of the paper to one long edge of the spine and press it gently into position (52A). Fold back over the spine and crease it exactly down the edge (B). Fold twice more (B, C) and slit the last fold with a knife to remove the excess. Slide the paper off the spine, reglue the spine and place the centre portion of the paper onto the spine (D). Damp the portion on the spine and rub it down. Fold in the two strips from either side, the unglued

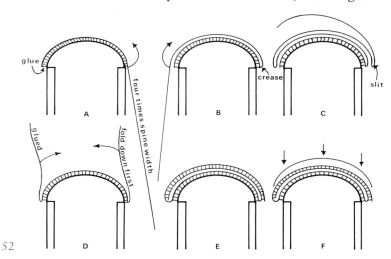

52

portion first (E). A further single strip glued on top will stiffen the hollow, providing one layer stuck to the spine and three stuck together, off the spine (F). The usual second lining (80) may be omitted when a hollow is made but it is an advantage with large, thick volumes.

11
Headbanding

The inserted cord or sewn headbands, at both head and tail, serve to support the sections by filling in the space between the spine of the sections and the board edge (the squares). Extra strength is also necessary because many readers will remove a book from a shelf by hooking a finger over the headcap (17) and pulling, instead of first pushing back the two volumes on either side and taking out the book by its middle. In early bindings the headbanding was an integral part of the section sewing and the core was made of stout twists of pigskin, whose ends were laced into the tops of the boards. As books became smaller and binding methods more refined, the cerf was introduced and headbands were sewn separately. These then degenerated for the sake of economy to machine-embroidered headbands, which were simply stuck to the spine and served no other purpose than decoration. Invariably these false headbands (105) are not equal to the squares (17), are limp and cannot support the sections.

The core for modern headbands, which are rectangular and on which the thread is embroidered, is a piece of thin vellum backed with leather. Prepare several pieces of different thicknesses, and cut strips from them, to the same width as the squares on the book and 25mm longer than the round of the spine. Thin books should have thinner cores so that movement of the sections is not restricted. (As rectangular headbands were unknown in early books, a round core of woven natural-fibre cord would be in character for this type of work. This would have been sewn with linen thread, with the alternating thread dyed the traditional blue, green or red.) Use cotton or linen embroidery thread of the corded variety. Silk is not recommended as it has a limited life. Single-core headbands are used for elementary work, and it is an affectation to sew a double or treble headband on any except large books with deep squares. Alternatively, cord may be inserted within the spine turn-in of cloth-bound and leather-covered books and is preferable to ready-made headbands (88). The colours of sewn headbands should harmonize with the tones of the covering material and endpapers. Two colours, brightly contrasting (e.g. royal blue and gold) are effective, and one colour alone can be subtle and attractive. A variation might be one bright colour with a few loops of another colour in the centre. Tie-downs should be frequent (see below) and the band must sit firmly on the edge of the spine to be supported by the first and second linings. Joins in the thread are made on the back using a weaver's knot when it is necessary to lengthen the thread or change its colour (31). Headbands begin and end a little short of the round of the spine, as this will facilitate forming the headcap when covering.

Sewing a single headband

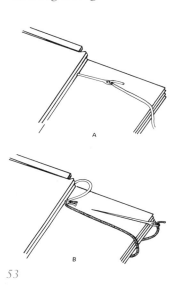

53

A finishing press is required for this operation. For simple explanation a black and white thread is described. Cut the core as explained above. Thread two long, slender needles, one with white thread and the other with black; the white thread should be about a third longer than the black. (Try to estimate the length of thread accurately, as extra thread will fray and become grubby, while too little will result in a join having to be made.) Tie the two threads together at one end, cut the excess off close to the knot and flatten this with a bone folder. Open the book to about the first four leaves beyond the endpapers. Push the 'white' needle between the leaves, through the joint and immediately beneath the kettle stitch (53A). Pull the thread from the outside of the section until the knot stops in the joint. Push the needle through the same hole again, the same way, to leave a loose loop of thread (53B). Hold the book by the tail/foredge corner in the finishing press. Put the core inside the loop and pull the thread tight, holding the core upright and flush with the back edge of the spine. Keeping the white thread taut, bring it up from the back and over the core, making a second loop alongside the first (53C). Now take the black thread under the core on the right of the white loops and pass it tightly around to form a 'bead' at the base of the two white threads (53D). Holding it tight against the white threads, loop it twice over the core, laying each thread closely beside the previous one (53E). Holding both threads taut, cross the white over the black to make another bead, then round the core to make further loops as before. Repeat this with the black thread. Now make a tie-down as follows: push the white needle down inside the book alongside the last black loop (53F, G) and direct the needle through the section at such an angle that it emerges from the spine immediately under the kettle stitch. Pull the needle through. Pull both threads so that the white bead tightens across the black loops on the surface of the book. Continue with the white for two loops, cross over with the black to make a bead. Make two loops with the black and cross over with the white. Continue this procedure along the core without overlapping the

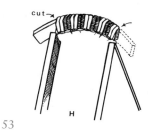

threads, securing the core with tie-downs at every other set of white loops. Finish the headband a little short of the round of the spine. It is immaterial what colour finishes, but at the last loop push the needle inside the book, and push it out below the kettle stitch. Cross over with the other thread to make the last bead and take it down at the same place, but push it out above the kettle stitch. Tie the two ends together with a reef knot across the kettle stitch and cut off all but 12mm of the excess thread (53G). Rub glue under the tie-downs and on the knot and flatten both with a bone folder until they stick to the spine. Glue the first and last loops to the back of the core to hold them in place and cut away the excess core with a scalpel (53H).

12 Leather paring

This is often singled out as one of the most difficult skills in bookbinding, but students should not be apprehensive about it: all that is needed is confidence and sharp tools. Paring is essential in some styles to make the binding functional. It also provides elegance at the turn-in on covers and spine. For the beginner, it is necessary only to know how to pare for the library style, which is illustrated in 93. Only the minimum amount of leather is pared away. A book that opens on 'silken' hinges through over-pared leather is weak in construction and poor in craftsmanship. The exact amount pared varies according to the construction of the book and its size and weight, and also the type and thickness of the leather. Experience is the guide.

The following preparatory exercises will assist in controlling knives and leather. The tools required are:

paring knife (English knife illustrated, but French knife used in a similar way)
spokeshave
paring stone
G clamps
strop

Paring the edges

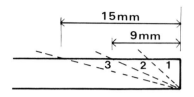

54. Exercises in edge paring

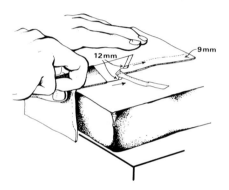

55. Edge paring: the second stage

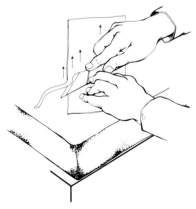

56. Edge paring: alternative method

The following exercise is done in three stages. Cut a strip of leather 100 × 225mm and draw two parallel lines around the edges, 9mm and 15mm away from them. Place the strip on the stone. Position the blade at 45 degrees to the edge (54:1). Push forward to remove a thin strip of leather and continue around all four edges. This first stage is known as the edge pare. The leather should come away cleanly without effort; if the edge is woolly the knife must be sharpened.

To achieve the second cut, use the part of the blade towards the heel and keep the tip clear of the surface. Mark the blade 12mm from the heel. Hold the strip of leather by one end against the edge of the stone with the thumb and spread it flat with the fingers (55). Beginning about 25mm in from the end of the strip, coincide the mark on the knife blade with the 9mm line on the leather. Adjust the blade angle to this line and push with the knife to remove the paring (54: 2). If the mark on the blade does not deviate from the line on the leather, if the pressure is even and the blade angle does not change, a clean cut will result.

The third paring is removed in the same way, the blade being marked 18mm from the heel to coincide with the 15mm line drawn on the leather (54:3). Pare all the edges in this manner.

Paring should be done in a continuous movement: the knife is never withdrawn but the leather pulled back as the knife advances. Only the end of the blade should rest on the stone, the hand stays clear of the edge of the stone and the knife is not raised. (If it were, the angle would change and the leather would be sliced through.)

An alternative method is shown in 56. The leather, after the first edge pare, is placed flat and in the middle of the stone and the knife held by the tips of the fingers. Using the middle of the knife blade, angle it to remove the second strip. Sweep the knife from one end to the other, holding the leather firm with the other hand. The third piece is pared by altering the angle of the blade.

The leather should now be extremely thin at the outside but reaching its full thickness 15mm from the edge. Erratic movements of the knife will result in uneven paring. Keep angles low, the knife tip clear and where possible the hands behind the blade.

Paring middle portions

This is done with the spokeshave (which is also used for reducing large areas for labels and onlays). Always edge-pare the leather first, otherwise the blade will catch the edge and rip the leather. G clamp the leather onto the stone, with a strip of soft card in between to prevent bruising. Position the clamp near the area to be pared (57), as excess movement of the strip will cause tearing. Move the spokeshave in a continuous, thrusting movement, continually changing the angle of direction to achieve evenness. At frequent intervals lift the leather and clear away the parings from underneath. If this is neglected, bumps will be sliced away.

57. The action of the spokeshave

The French knife can also be used, with a forward scraping action. G clamps are not used, and the strip is kept flat with the free hand.

In all paring, movements are deliberate, the knife is held firmly and every cut is controlled by an automatic directive from the mind. In this way a successful result is achieved and safety observed. All knives and blades must be keen and should be sharpened constantly on the strop. Evenness of paring can be checked in most leathers by examining the evenness of the dye (which changes in tone through the leather). Patchy colour indicates uneven thickness caused by changes in the knife angle. To check both evenness and thickness of the pared leather, fold it and run the fingers firmly along the crease.

51

Finishing

58. 'Handle' letters and figures

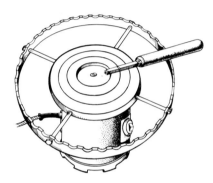

59. Finishing stove

60. Gold cushion and knife

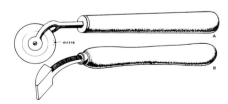

61. Fillet and polishing iron

A binding is most often judged by its appearance. The layman will look critically at the finishing – the brightness of the goldwork and the regularity of the title – but will have no appreciation of the skills expended in the forwarding. Although finishing adds nothing to the preservation of the contents, the book must be titled and the decoration should appeal to the senses. A commitment to the craft and determined practice are all that is required for successful finishing. Gold tooling, except in certain areas of the trade, is rarely lavished on the spines and sides of books. There is now a tendency towards simplicity and restraint. The reason for this is partly that the cost of gold work is uneconomic, and finishers unavailable, but it most probably above all reflects a change in taste.

Old decorative finishing tools are difficult to acquire and copies are expensive, but in order to restore antiquarian books a collection of them is essential. The beginner may achieve satisfactory results with the following finishing tools:

Finishing press (6)

Three sets of 'handle' (hand) letters and figures (58). These should be in a Roman face (with serifs) in 8, 12 and 16 point sizes.

Finishing stove (59)

Gold cushion (60). A wooden base padded with cotton wool and covered with suede leather, on which the gold leaf is cut. A strip of coarse leather is pasted on at one end for cleaning and polishing the faces of the tools.

Gold knife (60). A flat-bladed knife with a blunted edge. This is used to cut the gold leaf.

Two single-line fillets (61A) 1mm and 0.5mm.

Polishing iron (61B).

Two single-line pallets (62A) 1mm and 0.5mm.

Two decorative pallets (62B).

Six decorative hand tools (62C). It is wise to choose simple units, such as leaf forms, that can be used singly

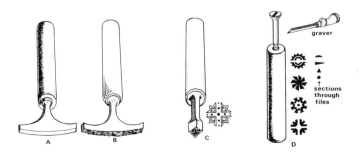

62. Single-line pallet (A), decorative pallet (B), and hand tools (C,D)

or built up as a composite pattern. Home-made tools can be highly satisfactory and much pleasure gained in creating them. Any piece of brass held in a wooden handle and able to retain heat can be used (100mm brass screws are ideal) and can be shaped with needle files, drills and metal gravers (62D).

Sundries

Gold leaf. 22 carat with 2 carats of silver, beaten by machine to a thinness of 1/250,000 inch. Sold in book form and interleaved with tissue for protection.

Gold foil. Paper or plastic film coated electronically with gold and backed with a sticking medium that reacts to heat. Invented in 1932, it made possible the economic titling of books produced by machine. Sold in ribbon form, the most practical width being 25mm.

Imitation gold foil. A substitute, made of gold-coloured aluminium; used only for ephemeral bindings.

Coloured foil. Coated film available in all pigment and metallic colours.

Gold rubber. Pure rubber rendered to a plastic consistency by drops of paraffin. It is used to remove excess gold leaf after tooling.

Cotton wool (US: cotton). Used to apply vaseline to the leather.

Vaseline. A grease harmless to leather, used to adhere the gold leaf to the leather before tooling.

Cooling pad. A pad of cloth soaked in a container of water and used to cool finishing tools to the temperature required.

Glaire. A medium that sticks the gold permanently to leather on application of heat. Natural glaire is one part egg white, one part water and half a part of vinegar. The mixture is shaken, left to stand for an hour then strained through fine muslin. (Alternatively, egg white crystals can be purchased and mixed in the proportion of one part crystals to four parts water. It is left until dissolved and then strained.) Both preparations will deteriorate in a few days, so it is wise to mix small quantities. Synthetic glaire is produced from shellac and is a comparatively recent innovation. The liquid does not deteriorate and makes the preliminary paste washing used with organic glaire unnecessary. One coat only is applied and the tool used at a very low temperature. Tooling is still possible some weeks after application. Some finishers have reservations about the results, but the student should decide for him- or herself which glaire is most suitable.

Gold tooling

It is always important to choose leather prepared for bookbinding, whose surface has not been artificially grained or coated with dressing. Gold work will be more successful on wet days because of the humidity in the air, but also depends on good forwarding.

Tooling with gold foil

Foil is ideal for tooling on cloth and rexine, as no wet preparations are involved, which might spoil the fabric. On coarsely woven cloth only large letters can be used, whereas very smooth cloth will take small letters quite well.

Three principles are involved when working with foil: heat, pressure and 'dwell' (the length of time the tool remains on the material). Should the tool be very hot, the pressure should be light and the dwell instantaneous. If, on the other hand, the tool is cool, the impression should be firmer and the dwell longer. The tool, in any case, should be heated to a slightly higher temperature than is required, then cooled to the correct working temperature. A series of trials should be made to discover the correct combination, particularly as different foils and covering materials react in different ways.

How to tool

First practise on bank paper as follows. Scratch a line with a pair of dividers on the paper. Select a large alphabet (16 point size) of hand letters and, using the tools cold, make impressions with all the letters on the paper, working on but *under* the lines. (This allows a clear view for spacing the letters correctly and placing them upright.) Hold the tool firmly in the fist with the thumb on top of the handle (63). The nick in the shaft should face towards the top of the work, to indicate that the letter is the right way up. The shaft of the tool must be held absolutely vertical and the face of the tool a few millimetres from the surface. Pause to get the tool in position, guiding it with the thumbnail, and 'strike' the tool with a firm but slight north-south-east-west movement with the fist. (This will ensure that the whole face of the tool has made contact with the paper.) If the impressions are crooked or uneven, continue to practise with the whole alphabet until satisfied. Now choose the required initials, impress them carefully on paper, and cut them out, leaving a 9mm margin all round. Glue some cloth onto a piece of card for preliminary trials. Attach the letters to the cloth with adhesive tape and slip a piece of gold foil (the sticking medium side down) beneath the paper. Heat the tools on the stove, but do not let them overheat as the shafts will char the handles. Pick up the first hand letter and place its shaft *only* on the cooling pad momentarily to reduce the temperature. Touch a spot of water near the top of the shaft; if it splutters, it is too hot and should be cooled again. The water should evaporate slowly, and the tool used

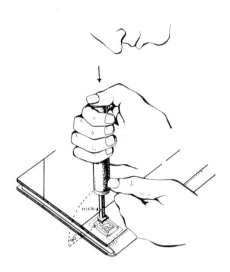

63. Using handle letters

immediately it reaches this point. Grip the tool as before and, using the paper impressions as a guide, pause, strike through the paper to impress the gold letters onto the cloth (63). Remove the paper and used foil. Should the negative parts of the letters be filled with gold, this indicates that the tool was too hot. If the impressions are vague and the gold broken, either the tool was too cool or it was not held vertically and the north-south-east-west movement incorrect. The broken letters may be completed thus: rest the heated tool in the impression, tilt the face up from the missing portion and slip foil underneath, bringing the tool down firmly with a bias towards the missing part. Surplus gold around the letters can be removed with a soft pencil eraser. If the trials are successful, work on the book itself, in the same way.

Coloured foils are tooled using the same method.

Tooling with gold leaf

The student should start with Method 1 and progress to Method 2 only when he or she has gained confidence through frequent practice.

Method 1 (with paper template)

First impress the required letters on bank paper as for foil. Attach the template to the leather with adhesive tape and impress the letters with hot tools through the paper to make 'blind' impressions (i.e. without gold or colour). At this stage, remove the tools from the stove, to avoid overheating. If using organic glaire, fill the grain of the leather with a paste wash by wiping this over the surface with cotton wool. This will prevent the glaire sinking below the surface. (Morocco requires a thin wash of milky consistency, but for calf and hides it should be a little thicker.) When it is dry, carefully paint the blind impressions with glaire, using a fine brush. Leave to dry and then apply a second coat to ensure that the surface is covered. Leave to dry, and do not be impatient to begin tooling as wet leather will cinder if hot tools are applied. (The rule to follow here is that when the glaire appears to be dry, it should be left for another five minutes.) While the glaire is drying, place the lettering tools on the stove in order of use.

As gold leaf is vulnerable to grease and draughts, the following method of handling is advised to prevent waste: polish the gold knife vigorously on the pad and do not touch the blade or cushion. Place the book of gold at one end of the cushion, and with finger and thumb lift all but the last tissue with its leaf of gold. Gently tap this tissue, close to its edge, with the flat side of the knife. The slight draught will cause the leaf to rise. Slip the blade under the gold at its centre. Raise the knife and turn it over, 'walking' the tip and moving the leaf until it lies flat on the pad. If it is crinkled or folded, blow sharply on its centre and it will lie flat. To cut the gold, hold the blade vertical and make short sawing actions on the pad. Assess the height of the letters and cut the gold a little more than this height and to a length of about 15mm. Cut as much as required, separate these pieces from the remainder, which should then be covered with a box. Now prepare the leather for tooling, as follows. Take a little vaseline on a pad of cotton wool and rub over the back of the hand to distribute the grease evenly. Rub the pad over the area to be lettered. Shape another pad of cotton wool to the size of the pieces of gold. Stroke the side of the nose with this pad. (This will provide enough grease to pick up the individual pieces of gold.) Transfer them to the vaselined impressions. Apply a second layer of gold immediately, without vaseline, and firm it down with gentle dabs of the cotton wool. Shade the gold with the hand to check for cracks and cover these with further pieces of gold. Tool immediately, using the same heat and movement as for foil (see above). The blind impressions will provide a sufficient guide to placing the tools. (If in doubt about the positioning, shade or change the light source for a clearer view.) Do not press too hard as the letter shapes may become distorted. On completion of the titling, rub over the letters with a gold rubber to remove surplus gold. A blurred, 'cooked' appearance on the letters indicates that the tools were too hot or the preparations not dry. Incomplete letters indicate that the tools were too cool or the pressure not even. If this is so, cut small pieces of gold to cover the missing portions and put them on without vaseline. When striking the tool for the second time feel the face slip into the previous impression and press with a bias towards the missing part. Should the result still be unsatisfactory, give the letter another coat of glaire and allow to dry. Apply vaseline and gold, and tool again. If excess gold remains in the grain of the leather, a little 'Robinol' (safe substitute for benzine) on a cotton wool pad will remove it.

The hot tool struck into the blind impression melts the vaseline and squeezes it to the sides, and the glaire, activated by the heat, fixes the gold. The resulting burnish can be brightened by tooling again without gold. Impressions are made more solid by tooling subsequent layers of glaire and gold, although this is uneconomic and often unnecessary. Gold remaining on the walls of the impression or filling the negative areas can be removed with a damp, pointed matchstick.

Method 2 (without paper template)

Paste wash and glaire the area to be tooled twice. Apply two layers of gold. Make fine guide lines on the gold by means of a length of thin sewing thread pulled in a see-sawing motion across the spine (64). Mark the centres of these lines lightly with dividers and tool the letters as in Method 1, working from the middle outwards, just *under* the guide lines. The disadvantages of this method are that much gold is wasted, and extra care must be taken in the spacing and positioning of the letters. It is not recommended for fine work involving complicated or small lettering, where paper patterns should be used.

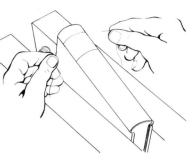

64. Making guide lines on gold leaf

Gold need not always be used: blind tooling looks splendid on light-toned leathers, for example. Blind lines (made as for gold tooling, but without the gold foil or leaf) can be intensified by burnishing with the heated tool. (Either a pallet or a fillet fixed with a wedge may be used, as in Project 5a; 127). Similarly, letters or decorative shapes can be darkened by first dampening the blind impressions and letting all the moisture disappear from the surface, and then applying a medium-hot tool. The touch should be instant, but as work progresses and the tool cools, the dwell may have to be longer to achieve the required depth of tone.

Using the fillet

Heat the fillet in the same way as the other tools, but test all sections of the wheel to make sure the heat is evenly distributed. With one hand, grip the base of the wooden handle and rest the other end on your shoulder. Stand firmly with one foot in front of the other and lean over the work. Pull the fillet towards the body, sight along the flat side of the wheel and guide it into position with your thumbnail. Lean on the handle and push the wheel with your body and not your arm. (Left-handed fillets have the wheel reversed in the holder to make sighting convenient.) The beginnings and ends of fillet lines are completed with a short pallet equal in thickness to the fillet (128).

A mitred fillet (61A) facilitates the execution of right angles, and can also be used for the ends of lines. To tool the end of a line, stop the fillet just short of the end, lift it and adjust the position of the cut-away portion to complete the line. Do not run the wheel backwards, as it is difficult to control. If a line longer than the circumference of the fillet is needed, stop short of the cut-out portion, lift the wheel and move it on, to continue the line.

Binding design

Half bindings with corners (see p.26) do not lend themselves to decoration, but those with foredge strips open up possibilities for creative design (using gold leaf

57

on leather and foil on cloth and paper; 126). Although decoration is not usually lavished on half bindings, additional bindings similar to Project 5 may be tooled, to give the student experience. Paper patterns drawn to the exact size of the cover are used to place lettering and complicated decoration on fine work. Front and back designs can be linked across the spine to make a harmonious whole.

Library bindings covered in leather should show the necessary information for reference and storage (see Project 7a; p.85), but personal books need not be so conventional, and with imagination the covers can be made attractive with gold and blind tooling (125,126).

Polishing

The final stage of finishing is polishing. Traditionally, fine bindings were 'plated' by subjecting the cover to sustained pressure between polished metal plates. The result was a hard, glossy appearance which is unpopular today. The use of plastics to simulate leather has turned opinion to favour the natural look and feel of leather, and polishing is now kept to a minimum.

How to polish

First rub over the leather with a damp sponge to remove finger or paste marks, and leave it to dry. Heat the polishing iron to a little above the temperature for gold tooling and hold it slightly away from you, keeping your upper arm close to your body. Maintain pressure to steady the tool and add to the weight of the iron. Use small, circular movements, using the face of the tool, and move gradually over the leather (65). Do not tip the tool, or score marks will occur. Siding material (decorated paper, etc.) should be protected with paper.

An alternative method, which avoids crushing the grain by heat and pressure, makes use of an ordinary bristle nail brush. Lightly dampen the leather and let all signs of moisture disappear, then brush it vigorously until it shines. The gold will not be damaged if it was applied correctly, but it may be necessary to restore some blind tooling.

The life of the book will be extended if the leather is rubbed over with British Museum leather dressing (see list of suppliers, p.94) or equal parts of lanolin and neatsfoot oil mixed together. Use very, very little and leave it for a few hours before polishing with a soft cloth.

An artificial glaze given to leather by a coat of varnish is harmful. Eventually the varnish will darken and yellow; it will crack at the hinges and prevent the leather from absorbing natural grease from the hands.

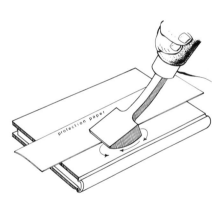

65. The action of the polishing iron

Part Two
Projects

The following projects have been divided into two parts: forwarding and finishing. This follows the traditional practice of completing the forwarding on a batch of books before starting the finishing processes, as an entirely different set of tools and skills are involved. The student is urged to repeat each forwarding project until a satisfactory result has been obtained. In the early stages, do not be too concerned with finger-marks, misplaced glue and materials out of square, as these will be corrected with familiarity and experience, and the resulting faulty bindings can in any case be used to practise the titling and decorating. The finishing projects relate directly to those for forwarding, and both have been planned in order of difficulty so that the student will acquire skills in the use of equipment and materials. It will be beneficial to read the theory chapters in Part I first, for a complete understanding of the processes, before forwarding and finishing are attempted.

In the first three projects, a full list of materials is given, but it is assumed that thereafter the student will have built up a stock and so will have the more frequently used materials to hand.

Forwarding

Project 1 Single-section (16-page) pamphlet binding, quarter bound in cloth (*or* whole binding)

Three-hole thread sewn

Folded round endpapers

Boarded (i.e. having stiff covers)

Decorated paper sides

Cut flush (i.e. both sections and cover cut the same size)

Materials

One sheet of white cartridge paper, or equivalent, crown size (or A2), for the section

Two sheets of coloured Abbey Mill paper, or equivalent, 7 ½ × 10. in (or A4), for endpapers

One piece of mull, 25mm shorter than the length of the section, and at least 75mm wide, to reinforce the join of the book to the boards

Glue (hot or cold) and glue brush

Waste paper

Bookbinder's needle

Thread, 16/2 or equivalent

Two pieces of 1000 gsm strawboard for front and back boards, 7½ in. (or 297mm) long, and 9mm less than the section in width. (Ensure that the grain runs from head to tail.)

Pencil

Shears

Two strips of 1000 gsm strawboard, 9mm wide and longer than 7½ in. (or 297mm)

Set square

Carpenter's square

Millboard, for use in cutting

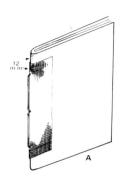

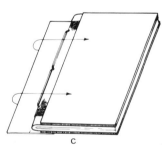

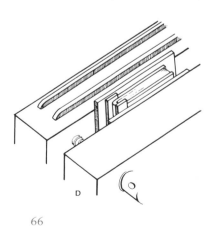

66

Knife
Bookcloth (enough for quarter binding or whole
 binding, as appropriate; 24)
Two pieces of decorated paper (see pp.27-29) for siding
Larger bone folder

Method

Fold the crown sheet to crown octavo (or A2 to A5) as
on p.23 (ensuring that the grain direction runs from
head to tail), to give a 16-page section. Wrap the
coloured sheets round the section to form endpapers, as
in 27C, again ensuring that the grain runs from head to
tail. Put the section between pressing boards in the
nipping press and apply pressure for ten minutes to
consolidate it. Apply glue to a piece of waste paper, lay
the mull onto it and run the fingers lightly over the
surface to ensure that the glue is spread evenly. (This
will provide enough glue for it to stick without mess.)
Peel off the mull and lay it, glued side uppermost, on the
bench. Position the spine of the section centrally on the
mull and wrap the mull around the section, smoothing it
with the fingers. (66A).

Sew the book with the three-hole method, as on p.38,
judging the position of the stitches by eye. Apply glue to
the boards and position them 9mm from the back fold,
lining them up to the head of the section (66B). Press the
book for a few seconds in the nipping press, between
pressing boards. Mark a quarter of the width of the
book on the front board and the same on the back, as in
24. Wrap a slip of paper round the book between these
two marks to ascertain the width of cloth required. (The
length will be the same as that of the book.) Cut a paper
template to this size so that the bookcloth can be cut out
without error. Cut the cloth with the warp threads in the
long direction, and mark a pitch line down the middle,
on the under side. Place the cloth on waste paper, glue it,
then transfer it to the bench. Position the spine of the
book on the pitch line, wrap the cloth onto the sides and
model it to the book and boards with hand pressure and
a bone folder (66C). Some cloths will bruise if rubbed
too hard with a folder, so protect the work with strong
paper.

Cut the two pieces of decorated paper to the length of
the book and wide enough to cover the exposed boards.
Apply glue to the under sides. Cover the sides with
them, binding down (i.e. just covering) the extreme
edges of the cloth. This operation is known as 'siding'. If
you are not sure that the paper has stuck properly, nip
the book in the press between boards for a few seconds.

Order of operations

1 Fold paper to a 16-page section
2 Fold endpapers and wrap round section
3 Press
4 Cut and glue on mull
5 Sew
6 Cut and attach boards
7 Press
8 Make template for covering cloth
9 Cut cloth
10 Glue on cloth
11 If quarter binding, side with decorated paper
12 Press
13 Mark up for cutting
14 Cut edges
15 Leave to dry under weighted boards

Mark up for cutting the edges, as explained on p.40 (36). Follow the instructions for cutting, but without using cutting boards. Instead, two strips of strawboard should be positioned at the hinges when trimming head and tail so the book is 'solid' in the press and the edges cleanly cut (66D). Leave to dry under weighted pressing boards.

This exercise can also be carried out as a whole binding in cloth, as follows. After the boards are attached and the book has been in the nipping press, make a template for the cloth by lining the book up against two corner edges of waste paper, wrapping the paper round the book and marking off the correct size on the paper. Cut the cloth from this template. Apply glue to the cloth, pitch the book to the top and one side edge, wrap the cloth around the book and model it to the hinge and boards with a folder.

Note that glue is used throughout the work rather than paste. Its low water content controls the stretching of both cover and endpapers equally. This equal pull ensures that the book will be flat when dry, providing the grain of all materials runs from head to tail.

Project 2 Single-section (16-page) pamphlet binding, quarter bound in cloth

Five-hole thread sewn

Folded round endpapers

Boarded

Decorated paper sides

Cut flush, turned in all round (i.e. the cloth extends to the inside of the binding, covering the raw edges of the boards)

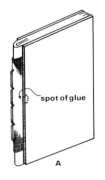

spot of glue

A

67

Materials

As for Project 1.

Method

Prepare a section with endpapers, including mull, as in Project 1, but sew it with the five-hole method, as explained on p.38 (35C). Cut the boards as in Project 1, but secure them with a mere touch of glue half-way down the inner back edges of the boards (67A). Mark up for cutting, and trim the edges as on pp.41-42. Make a template for a quarter binding as in Project 1, but extend the length by 30mm (15mm each at head and tail) to allow for the turn-in. Cut the cloth and glue it to the book and boards as in Project 1. Open the book at the centre and lay it flat on the bench, as in 67B. Lift up the section at head and tail, turn the extra cloth over the edges of the boards and stick it to the inside. More glue may be applied to secure the turn-in if necessary. Smooth this turn-in with a folder to remove any creases. Cut decorated paper as in Project 1, but allow 15mm extra at the foredge and 15mm each for the turn-in at head and tail. Glue and pitch the paper as in Project 1. Cut the corners of the overlap at 45 degrees before turning them in (67C). Mould the material to the edge of the board with a folder (67D). (Tunnels left between board edges and covering will wear rapidly and expose

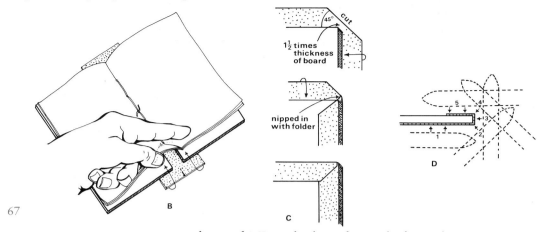

67

B

C

D

Order of operations

1 Fold paper to 16-page section
2 Fold endpapers and wrap round section
3 Press
4 Cut and glue on mull
5 Sew
6 Cut and attach boards with spot of glue
7 Mark up for cutting
8 Cut edges
9 Make template for covering cloth
10 Cut cloth
11 Glue on cloth
12 Side with decorated paper
13 Put down endpapers
14 Leave to dry under weighted boards

the card.) Free the boards gently from their initial glued positions and lay them flat. Place a sheet of waste paper under the front board paper. Apply glue to the board paper and remove the waste. Shut down the front board. Repeat this procedure with the back board. Rub down the joint with a folder to set the cloth to the board paper and, without opening the book, place it between pressing boards and nip in the press for a few seconds. Remove it from the press and examine it. If the endpapers stretch beyond the foredge, this could indicate either slow working, very thin glue or flimsy endpapers, and can be obviated in later attempts by removing a narrow strip from the foredge of the endpaper before gluing. The amount trimmed should equal the stretch of the paper, but can only be judged by familiarity with adhesives and paper substance. Finally, leave the book to dry between weighted boards.

Project 3 Single-section (32-page) pamphlet binding, half bound in cloth (*or* whole cloth binding)

Five-hole thread sewn

Tipped on endpapers

Boarded

If half bound, decorated paper sides

With squares (i.e. with a margin between the edge of the paper and the edge of the board)

Materials

As for Project 1, except:

Two sheets rather than one of cartridge paper, crown size (or A2)

Two sheets rather than one of Abbey Mill paper, 7½ × 10 in (or A4) for endpapers

Instead of mull, one piece of thin bookcloth or jaconette 25mm less than the length of the section and 75mm wide, to reinforce the spine

1400 gsm strawboard (rather than 1000 gsm) sufficient for front and back

Bookcloth (enough for either a half binding with corners or foredge strips; *or* enough for a whole binding; see below and p.26)

Glue (hot or cold)

Glue brush

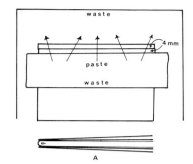

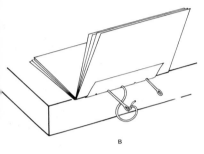

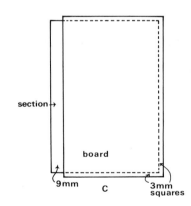

Straight-edge
Two pieces of decorated paper for siding

Method

Fold two 16-page sections as on p.23 and inset one within the other. Press for ten minutes. Cut two coloured 4-page endpapers and tip them onto the back edges using paste, as in 68A. Rub them down or nip them in the press to make certain they are stuck. Position the bookcloth or jaconette centrally round the section and place it on the edge of the bench with half the section vertical (68B). Hold it firmly and pierce five holes with a stout needle, leaving another needle in the last hole to retain the sheets in position while sewing, as in 35B. Judge all distances by eye and take care to sew exactly through the folds so as not to pierce the endpapers. Mark up for cutting and trim the edges (see pp.40-42).

Cut two boards for front and back, 9mm less from the back fold of the section and extending for 3mm at head, tail and foredge (68C). These must be square. (For most work this 3mm is standard, but squares can be smaller or larger depending on the size and weight of the book. The text is then protected but the squares are not so large that the board edges are not supported by the bulk of the sections.) Place the boards accurately, without adhesive, on the section and, without moving the positions of the boards, make a template for the covering of the spine as in Project 2 (extending the length by 30mm). Cut templates for the corners, whose diagonal bisecting lines should be equal to a quarter of the width of the book, with turn-ins of 15mm (68D). Cut the cloth for the spine and four corners. Mark a pitch line down the middle of the spine cloth. At this stage mark the front and back endpapers and boards 'F' and 'B' (for front and back) so that they can be distinguished later on. Position both boards again on the section, 9mm in from the spine and extending 3mm on the other three sides, then place the book on the edge of the bench so it can be lifted without moving the boards. Glue the cloth with thin glue. (A common fault is to use thick glue. Its 'instant grab' prevents the boards from being manipulated. As the cold-type glue sets much more slowly, it is much easier to use in this project.)

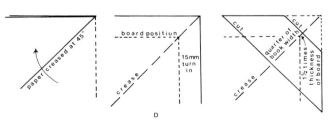

68

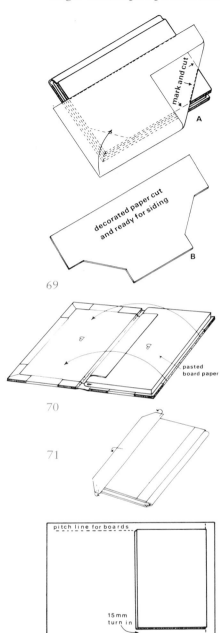

69

decorated paper cut
and ready for siding

70

71

pitch line for boards

15 mm
turn in

72

Order of operations

1 Fold and inset two 16-page
   sections
2 Press
3 Fold two 4-page coloured
   sheets for endpapers and tip
   them on
4 Cut reinforcing bookcloth or
   jaconette
5 Sew
6 Mark up for cutting

Continue as follows. Pick up the book and place the spine centrally on the pitch line, again on the edge of the bench, and wrap the cloth onto the sides as before. Put the section aside and complete the sticking of the cover, by turning in the overlaps at head and tail and running a folder firmly against the inner edges of the boards to seal down the cloth. Check accuracy by laying a straight-edge across the top edge of one board: the other board should also touch along the straight-edge. If it does not, the case is out of square and should be discarded. If adhesion is doubtful, nip the case in the press briefly. Glue the cloth corners, one at a time, as follows: pitch the board onto the cloth with equal turn-ins and model the cloth to the board with a bone folder as in 67D. Cut decorated papers for siding, wide enough to bind down the edge of the cloth and extending on three sides by 15mm. Hold the front paper in position and fold back the corners, creasing them ready to cut (69A). Remove, cut to shape as in 69B and mark with an 'F'. Cut the back paper in the same way and glue both in position.

The final operation, 'casing in', is done as follows. Lay the case face down on the bench. Place a waste sheet under the front board paper and apply paste to the paper and reinforcing cloth. Remove the waste, pick up the section and pitch it onto the case, with the edges 3mm from the head, tail and foredge. Without hesitation, place another waste sheet beneath the back board paper and paste cloth and paper as before. Remove the waste. Raise the section and the front board and turn both onto the back board, making sure both boards are aligned (70). Model the cloth at the hinge to make it stick to the section and, without opening the book, nip it in the press under light pressure. After ten seconds remove it and examine it for excess paste and other faults. Leave it to dry under weighted boards.

Instead of corners, foredge strips can be made as a variation. Glue and position the strips as in 71, cutting off the corners before turning in. This method of siding is both attractive and simple, and the paper is cut to bind down the edges of the cloth.

The book can also be covered completely in book-cloth. Make a paper template by positioning the section within its boards 15mm away from two corner edges of waste paper. Wrap the paper round the book, allow 15mm for turn-ins at the other two edges, and cut the cloth from the pattern. Place one board on the cloth 15mm from three edges. Line up a ruler with the head and draw two pitch lines as in 72. Place the section accurately between its boards and lay it aside. Apply glue to the cloth. Pick up the whole book without disturbing the boards and pitch it to the line drawn on the right of the cloth and to the top. Draw the left side of

7 Trim edges

8 Cut boards

9 Cut templates for cover

10 Cut cloth

11 Glue on cloth spine and corners, or cover in whole cloth

12 If a half binding, side with decorated paper

13 Put down endpapers ('casing in')

14 Press

15 Leave to dry under a weight

the cloth over it without the top board moving out of position. Immediately remove the section. Check that both boards are lined up with the top pitch line and that the gap between the boards at the spine is equal all the way down. Cut off the corners and turn in the overlapping cloth. Nip in the press for a few seconds. The case is now ready for casing in, as above.

Note that paste is used for the endpapers, as its water content will cause the board paper to stretch more, counteracting the pull of the covering material and 'bowing' the thicker boards towards the book.

Project 4 Multi-section address book; whole cloth case binding

Sewn on two tapes

Tipped-on endpapers

Boarded, with a flat back

Index

Materials

Nine sheets of ledger paper, crown size (or A2), for the sections

Two sheets of coloured paper, 7½ × 10 in. (or A4), for endpapers

Thread, 16/2 or equivalent

Two tapes, 12mm wide and 60mm long

Cutting pad (a pile of single sheets of waste paper cut the same size as the sections, to equal the swell)

1400 gsm strawboard, sufficient for the front and back boards and spine strip (see below)

Mull for the first lining

Kraft paper for the second lining

Bookcloth

Linen or thinly pared leather for strengthening the tabs, if desired

Method

Fold nine 16-page sections and press them for two hours in the nipping press. Tap the sections on the bench until they are aligned ('knocking up square') and screw them in the finishing press. Use a carpenter's square to check that the head is at right angles and all the sections are level, and mark up for sewing (33). Follow the sewing instructions on p.37, using the 'all along' method, with two tapes. It is not necessary to use a frame in this case, as few sections are involved. Work instead at the edge of the bench. Pull the tapes tight between the sections.

Tip on the 4-page endpapers as in 68A, with paste, lining them up to the edges of the first and last sections. Leave them under a weight to dry with the tapes 'outside'. Mark guide lines on the endpapers for cutting, as on p.40. Place the sections on the edge of the bench and apply glue to the spine, stippling it on with the

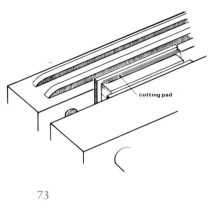

73

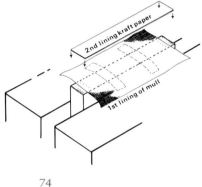

74

brush between the sections. Immediately lift the book and knock the spine and head firmly on the bench to level the sections (46). Cut the foredge as on p.41. Before cutting the head and tail, fan out a cutting pad, and place it as in 73. This will compensate for the swell in the spine caused by the sewing thread. The book is then 'solid' and the spine will not be crushed in the press. Cut the head and tail as on p.41. Cut two boards of 1400 gsm, 6mm less at the spine and extending 3mm beyond the head, tail and foredge. Cut a stiffener for the spine from the same board, to the same length as the boards and the width of the sewn sections. Remember that all measuring should be done by eye. Position the sections between the boards and screw them up in a finishing press.

Apply first and second linings to the spine to reinforce it, as follows. (This is common to most books.) Cut a piece of mull 12mm less than the length of the spine and 60mm wide. Lightly glue the backs of the sections, position the mull centrally and rub it down. Cut kraft paper to the exact size of the spine, glue it, place it in position, dampen it and rub it down with a folder (74). Leave the book to dry.

Make a template for the covering cloth as follows. Set the book accurately between the boards and place all three on a sheet of waste paper, 15mm away from two corner edges. Stand the stiffener against the spine, wrap the paper round the book, mark off the 15mm for the turn-in on the other two sides, and cut out a template. From this, cut the cloth. Draw pitch lines across the top and down the right-hand side of the cloth, 15mm from the edges (72). With the boards in position, place the book on the edge of the bench so it can be easily picked up. Apply glue to the cloth. Place book and boards up to the pitch lines, stand the stiffener against the spine and wrap the cloth round the boards. Working quickly, remove the sections and ensure that both boards and stiffener are aligned at the head and that the stiffener is centrally placed between the boards. Cut off the corners of the cloth as in Project 3, turn in the overlaps, run the folder against the four inner edges of the boards as in 67D, and nip in the press. (It is important to familiarize oneself with this working procedure and so work quickly, as the adhesive may dry before the case can be completed. Diluted glue will give a longer working time.)

If the turn-ins are uneven, set a pair of dividers to the smallest margin, mark off all round, and trim off the excess with a knife and a straight-edge. Follow Project 3 for casing in, but paste the tapes and mull as well as the board paper. Press the book with the flat, stiff back just outside the pressing boards. Leave it to dry under a weight.

Working out and cutting the index

Discounting the first and last leaves (which will be attached to the endpapers), the seventy remaining leaves should be divided among the letters of the alphabet as follows: B, H, and S should have five leaves each, G, M, N, R and W four each, A, C, D, J, L, P and T three each, F, K and O two each, and E, I, Q, U, V, X, Y and Z one each. (This index is standard, but others can be worked out according to requirements.)

As a cutting guide, cut a strip of paper 50mm wide by the length of the leaf. Measure the length of the leaf and divide it by the number of indexes or 'tabs' required. Mark this depth down from the top of the right-hand edge of the cutting guide. Also write the letters of the alphabet, one under the other, down the left-hand side of the strip, and add their allotted number of leaves. The width of each tab should be sufficient to contain the gold letters, and is marked on the top edge of the cutting guide, to the right-hand side. (If each tab does not seem high enough, the index could be rearranged so that letters such as E and F, I and J, U and V share the same tab.)

Beginning at the second leaf, count the leaves for the letter A and place a piece of card underneath them. Measure with the guide the depth and width of the tab. Cut away the strips below the tab with a scalpel and straight-edge. Cross off letter A on the guide. Count the leaves for B, place the card underneath, measure with the guide the tab depth and width and cut the strips away as before. Cross off letter B. Continue until tab Z, which is not cut. The tabs may then be strengthened by covering them with linen or thinly pared leather. They are finally lettered in gold (see p.83).

Order of operations

1 Fold and press nine 16-page sections
2 Fold two 4-page coloured endpapers
3 Mark up for sewing
4 Sew
5 Tip on endpapers
6 Leave under weight to dry
7 Mark up for cutting
8 Glue spine and knock up square
9 Trim edges
10 Cut boards and stiffener
11 Cut and attach first and second linings
12 Make template for cover
13 Cut cloth
14 Make the case
15 Trim the turn-in if necessary
16 Case in
17 Press
18 Leave to dry under weighted boards
19 Cut and letter index
20 Cover tabs with linen or thinly pared leather, and then tool in gold (see p.83)

Project 5 Multi-section whole cloth case binding, with a hard back

Sewn on four tapes
Common made endpapers
Rounded and backed

Materials

One publisher's case binding, approx. 225 × 150 × 30mm, of good paper, wide margins and in a reasonable condition

Four sheets of white cartridge or Abbey Mill paper, larger when folded than the selected book, for endpapers

Two sheets of coloured Abbey Mill or Ingres paper, as above, for endpapers

Materials for repair, as required (pp.33-34)

Four tapes, 12mm wide and 100mm long

Equipment for rounding and backing, as on p.44

Enough 1800 gsm strawboard for the cover

Manilla card for a stiffener

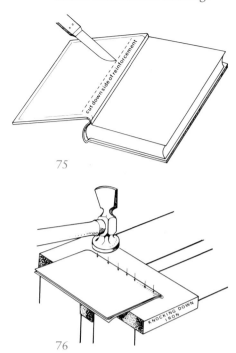

75

76

Order of operations

1 Collate book
2 Pull
3 Knock out old groove
4 Make endpapers
5 Repair and dry the sections
6 Press
7 Mark up for sewing
8 Sew
9 Tip on first and last sections and endpapers
10 Mark up for cutting and depth of joint
11 Glue spine and knock up
12 Cut foredge
13 Round and back
14 Cut head and tail
15 Cut boards and stiffener
16 Apply first and second linings
17 Make template for cover and cut cloth
18 Make case
19 Trim out case on inside
20 Prepare book for casing
21 Case in
22 Press
23 Form spine
24 Leave to dry

Mull and kraft for first and second lining, as in Project 4
Bookcloth
Two pieces of woven cord for the headcaps (see below)
Method
First collate the book (i.e. check that it is complete) before rebinding. Read Chapter 3 ('The Make-up of a Book') before 'pulling' the book (freeing the sections) as follows. Open the front cover and with a sharp knife cut along the edge of the reinforcing hinge visible under the board paper (75). Tear off the old fly leaf. Lever up the hinge and pull it outwards to loosen the linings from the first section. Count the number of leaves before the first stitching and cut the threads carefully. Count the same number of leaves, and this will indicate the number of leaves to the section. The next signature should be on the next page. Pull the first section free with an outward movement. Break away linings and glue from the second section, cut the stitching and remove it. Place it on top of the first section. Work thus through the whole book, freeing the leaves from bits of glue and thread, and keeping the sections in sequence as they are separated.

When pulling a book, it is essential to retain all the pages even if they are blank. Endpapers with signatures, written additions on fly leaves, book plates, booksellers' and binders' stickers should be retained, as they contribute to the history of the book.

All the sections except the middle ones will be bent at the back folds from the original backing, and this 'old groove' must now be removed, as follows (76). Fix the knocking-down iron at the end of the lying press, place the back fold of one section on it, cover it with a piece of tough paper for protection, and tap the fold with the hammer until it is flat. It is advisable to use the hammer in the middle of the knocking-down iron, and move the section.

Prepare the common made endpapers as on p.31 (27D).

Examine the outside folds of the sections for damage caused by pulling, by holding them to the light. If necessary, repair this and any other damage as in Chapter 6.

Collate and gather the sections and endpapers (which should be cut square at the head), knock them up square and put them between boards in the centre of the press for two days at intensive pressure. This pressing is important, as the true thickness of the book must be achieved before binding.

Mark up for sewing on four tapes as in 33. When cutting the cerf, avoid cutting into the endpapers, but bend them outwards away from the saw. Prepare a sewing frame (5) and sew the sections and endpapers all along, as on p.37. (Note the advice on swell and select the thread carefully; pp.34-35.) Tip on the first and last sections and paste the endpapers in position for 3mm (44). Mark up for cutting the edges. Draw a line the length of the section, near the spine, on both front and back, as a guide for the depth of joint. (As this is a case binding, the joint should be one and a half times the thickness of the board; see below). Apply glue to the spine and between the sections. Knock the book up square at the head and spine. Immediately cut the foredge, round and back, and trim the head and tail as explained on pp.41 and 43-45.

Cut two boards of 1800 gsm to fit in the joint and extending on all three sides for 3mm. Cut a stiffener of manilla card as long as these boards and as wide as the round of the book, measuring this with a piece of paper. Apply first and second linings as on p.66. Make a template for the cloth as in Project 4 and cut it. Cut two pieces of cord for inserting in the headcaps, as long as the round of the book and as wide as the squares. Place the sections between the boards, setting the squares equally on all three sides. Draw pitch lines on the cloth and glue it. Position the closed book on the cloth, place the stiffener against the spine and wrap the cloth round onto the top board as in Project 4. Immediately remove the sections, ensure that the stiffener is centred between the boards, place the cords at head and tail, cut off the corners of the cloth and turn in the edges. Use a folder to rub down the stiffener and mould the cloth against the inner edges of the boards (77). Nip in the press for two seconds and then examine for excess glue. Trim the turn-in equally all round.

Cut down the waste sheet of the endpapers at head and tail, and 25mm from the spine, to form a flange. Trim the mull and tapes neatly (78). Place a piece of waste paper under the back board paper and paste it, together with the flange, mull and tapes. Do not overpaste. Remove the waste paper and, taking all the sections, place the pasted side down in position against the inner edge of the boards, setting the squares and positioning the joint against the inner edges of the boards. Apply paste to the other endpaper, in the same way, and turn the top board over to fit in the joint, and align the boards. Do not open the book, but place it between boards, with the spine outside, and nip in the centre of the press. After ten seconds examine the book once more. Replace it in the press and use a folder to form the stiffener into a round shape (79). Leave the book to dry.

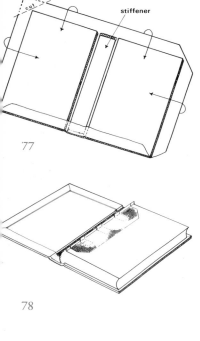

77

78

79

Project 6 Library-style binding in whole buckram, with a hollow back
Hidden cloth-jointed endpapers
Sewn on four tapes
Rounded and backed

Materials

At least three publisher's case bindings, as in Project 5
For each book:
    paper for endpapers
    board (mill- and strawboard)
    tape
    mull
    thread
    jaconette
    buckram
    kraft paper
    cord for headcaps
    manilla
    wax paper
    pair of plastic or non-ferrous knitting needles or similar rods, 4mm in diameter

This is an economical variation on the library style, being bound in buckram rather than leather, and is much in demand today. Although a sound binding material, buckram necessitates the use of the hollow back (see pp.45-47). The student is advised to study 80 for the constructional features of the library style and to attempt at least three books at the same time in order to gain proficiency in this advanced work.

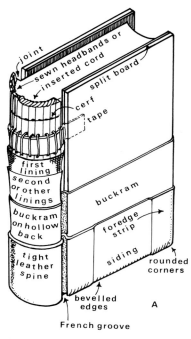

80

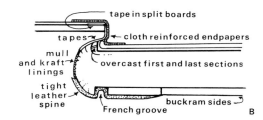

81. The French groove (B) compared with the flush joint (A), showing the use of thick leather at the hinge

Method

Collate, pull, knock out the old groove, repair as in Project 5, and press the books for one week. Prepare the hidden cloth-jointed endpapers as in 27F. Mark up the sections for sewing on four tapes, and sew the book and endpapers on a frame, using the all along method if possible (see p.37). Tip on the first and last sections and endpapers for 3mm. Mark up for cutting and for the depth of the joint. (The latter will be equal to the thickness of the split boards used.) Glue the spine and knock the sections square. Cut the foredge (p.41). Round and back (pp.43-45). Cut the head and tail (pp.41-42).

Cut the boards from 2.33mm millboard and 500 gsm strawboard 15mm larger than the book. The two boards when stuck together are, in thickness, equal to

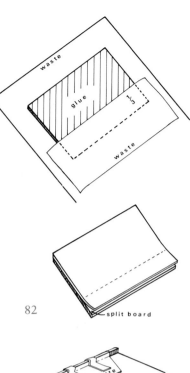

82

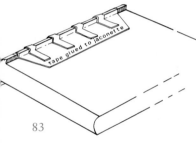

83

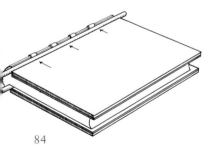

84

the depth of the joint. These 'split boards' are made as follows. Place a waste sheet to shield one third of the millboard and glue the remainder (82). Line up the thinner board to the unglued edge and press the two together. Nip them in the press.

Place one knitting needle in the joint, thrust the open edge of the board, millboard uppermost, against it, mark off squares of 3mm and cut the boards to size. The boards must be square and identical. (If a board chopper is not available, the boards can be cut together in the press and plough.)

Tear off the waste sheet of the endpapers and glue the tapes to the jaconette (83). Cut this to make a flange 25mm from the joint and 25mm from each end.

Glue the inside of the split board but keep the two parts separate. Position the rod against the joint and quickly slide the flange into the split. Set the edge of the board against the rod and check that the squares are equal all round (84). Do both sides quickly, remove the rods and nip the book in the press, leaving the groove and swell free. Examine the book to check that the boards are correctly positioned. Replace in the press and smother the spine with a layer of paste. After five minutes use the back of a knife to scrape it clean and remove excess glue. When the moisture dries out from the paste, the spine will be set in a permanent shape. (This operation, known as 'setting' the spine, is carried out on all advanced bindings.)

Apply first and second linings, both materials cut to the same size as the spine, and make a hollow back (52). Make a template for the covering cloth with an 18mm turn-in and 9mm extra on the width, to allow for the French groove. Cut the buckram and mark pitch lines at the head and down one edge. Prepare for covering by removing nubs of glue and 'softening' (very gently bevelling) the outside edges of the boards with sandpaper. Cut the free portion of the hollow down to the level of the boards and the attached part to the level of the sections. Slit the hollow on either side of the joints for 25mm to allow the cloth to be turned into it (85).

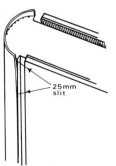

85

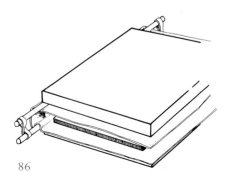

86

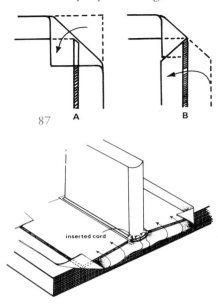

87   A   B

inserted cord

88

89

Order of operations

1 Collate and pull sections
2 Knock out old groove
3 Repair
4 Press
5 Make endpapers
6 Mark up for sewing
7 Sew
8 Tip on first and last sections and endpapers
9 Mark up for cutting and depth of joint
10 Glue spine and knock up
11 Cut foredge
12 Round and back
13 Cut head and tail
14 Make split boards and cut to size
15 Make flange
16 Attach boards
17 Set and clean spine
18 Apply first and second linings
19 Make hollow back
20 Make template for cover
21 Cut buckram

The operation of covering will be a lengthy one for the beginner, and work should be carried out without interruption, so at this point lay out bone folder, pressing boards and rods joined by elastic bands (86).

Cut two pieces of cord for the headcaps, as on p.69. As the adhesive may dry rapidly, soften the buckram first with paste to retain the moisture before gluing it. Apply glue to the outside of the hollow. Place the book on the pitch lines and draw the cloth around the book. Immediately push the blunt end of the folder into the French groove, clip the rods into the groove and nip the book in the press with pressing boards on the rods (86). Remove after one second and turn in the corners of the cloth only (87). Do not cut the cloth, but turn in the corners to make an efficient protection. (This method, which is not intended to be elegant, is known as the Universal Corner and is common in the library style; 89.) Lay the book to overhang the edge of the bench (88). Position the cord at the end of the hollow and bend both down. Turn in the cloth over the cord, into the hollow, between the joints and the spine, and mould it to the edges of the boards. Repeat for the other end. Turn in the cloth at the foredges (87B). Use a folder round the board edges and push the cloth into the French groove. Replace the rods and shape the headcaps (90). Without delay, nip the book in the press with the rods still in position. Examine the work for excess glue, etc., and leave it under a heavy weight to dry. Trim the excess turn-in on the inside of the covers, as in Project 4.

As a refinement, the exposed card can be 'filled in' with manilla or similar thin card equal to the thickness of the turn-in material, as follows. Place a piece of manilla larger than required against the inner edge of the board and run a hard pencil along the three edges of the turn-in, to make a sufficient mark for it to be cut out to fit (91). Glue it down. Sandpaper the bumps caused by the tape inside the split so that the board paper goes down smoothly, without the tapes or the turn-in showing. Put down endpapers 'shut', as follows. Place a sheet of waste under the board paper, paste the sheet, remove the waste and close the board on the book. Repeat for the other end. Without opening the book, nip

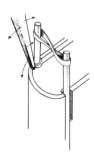

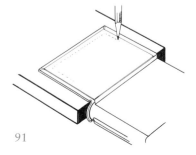

90   91

22 Prepare book for covering
23 Cover
24 Trim the inside
25 Fill in
26 Paste down endpapers
27 Press

it in the press for a few seconds. Examine it for excess paste, which should be wiped away, and a piece of wax paper inserted as protection before replacing the book in the press until it is dry. (Should the endpapers stretch excessively, cut off a narrow strip from the foredge before pasting, to make the squares even.)

Project 7 Library-style binding in half morocco
Tight backed
Exposed cloth-jointed endpapers
Sewn headbands
Buckram sides

Materials

Several case bindings, of various sizes and thicknesses Materials and equipment as for Project 6, plus enough morocco to cover the books as half bindings (24)

Working with leather

While working with leather, the student should proceed in an efficient but unhurried manner; paste may be kept active by dampening the leather with a sponge as necessary, or repasting. Some grained and dressed leathers are difficult to work and will need extra coats of paste. Pasted leather is easily moulded when wet, but will set permanently when dry. It is also vulnerable to uneven surfaces when wet, so remove rings and bracelets before starting work, wipe over all working surfaces to remove grit, trim your fingernails and handle the leather with the balls of the fingers only. Never press damp leather, as the grain will be crushed and become unsightly. Do not bring damp leather in contact with ferrous metal or it will be stained black.

Method

Repair any damaged parts (pp.33-34) and overcast the first and last sections of larger books to strengthen them before pressing (35F). Make the exposed cloth-jointed endpapers, as on p.32 (27G). Proceed with all the operations in Project 6 up to and including the attachment of the boards. (Double sew the endpapers as in 35H.) Make the flange by glueing the tapes to the waste sheet of the endpapers and cutting them to insert into the split board, as in Project 6. Set the back, as in Project 6. Sew single-core headbands as on pp.48-49. Reinforce the spine with the first and second linings (74), but continue these beyond the head and tail to support the headbands. The tight-backed library style should have a smooth spine (an uneven surface will soon wear), so sandpaper the second lining once it is dry (carefully, to avoid weakening the stitches), and glue another paper on top. If the back is still uneven and the spine wide enough, this paper may also be sandpapered and yet another layer applied. More than this will restrict movement in the spine and should be avoided.

73

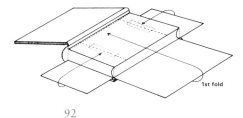

92

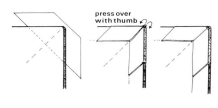

93

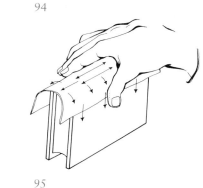

94

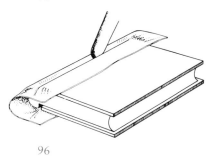

95

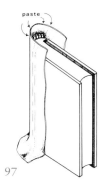

96

Prepare the book for covering, as follows. Trim the linings level with the headbands and bevel the edges of the boards with sandpaper. Envelop the sections in wax paper and fix this with adhesive tape as a barrier against paste and marks (92). Make templates for the covers and corners as in Project 3, allowing for a turn-in of 18mm.

Cut out the leather economically with a knife and straight-edge. Mark each book and its leather with the same symbol so that the correct leather is matched to each book. Pare the leather as on pp.49-51 (93). Attach the corners (or foredge strip) first, using two thin coats of paste. (Overpasting causes lumps beneath the surface.) Place them as in 94. Avoid rubbing the wet leather with a folder as this could bruise it, but use the fingers to model the corners so that they fit the boards tightly round the edges. Make certain the two angles of the corners meet precisely. (If necessary, draw the position of the corner on the outside of the board, with a 45-degree set square.) Examine the profile of the corners against a sheet of white paper and if the leather is uneven, tap it smooth with a folder. Wipe off excess paste and finger marks with a damp sponge and leave to dry.

Attach the spine leather as follows, working on a paring stone or any hard, clean surface. Paste the spine leather on some waste paper. Paste the spine of the book thinly and apply another coat to the leather. Centre the spine on the leather and rub it down firmly with the palm of the hand. Stretch any looseness or wrinkles down onto the sides (95). Push the blunt end of the folder along the French groove so that the gap does not close (96). At this stage, dampen the outside of the leather with water to prevent it drying out. Turn up the leather outwards at the tail and stand the book upright on the working surface. Put a little paste on the *outside* of the leather where it is to be turned in at the spine so that it will stick to the backs of the sections (97). Turn the overlap in on itself so the fold is level with the top of the headband, and pull the edges through the groove so that they can be stuck to the inside of the boards (98).

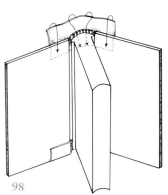

97

98

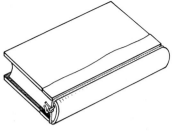

99

100

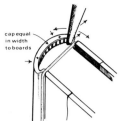

101

Order of operations

1 Collate and pull
2 Knock out old groove
3 Repair and overcast first and last sections
4 Press
5 Make endpapers
6 Mark up for sewing
7 Sew
8 Tip on first and last sections and endpapers
9 Mark up for cutting and the depth of joint
10 Glue spine and knock up square
11 Cut foredge
12 Round and back
13 Cut head and tail
14 Cut and make split boards
15 Make flange
16 Attach boards
17 Set the back
18 Sew headbands
19 Apply first, second and subsequent linings
20 Prepare book for covering and envelop with wax paper for protection
21 Make templates and cut leather
22 Pare
23 Attach corners
24 Cover and leave to dry
25 'Open' book
26 Trim leather on the outside
27 Side with buckram
28 Trim both leather and buckram inside
29 Fill in and sandpaper
30 Paste down endpapers
31 Press

102

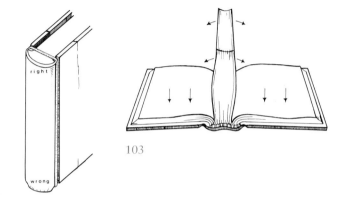

103

Mould the leather with the fingers to fit tightly. Turn in the tail in the same way and wipe the turn-ins free from paste before closing the boards. Rub the spine with the palm and push the folder once more along the French groove. Tie a loop of soft cotton string in the groove, knotting it between the boards (99). Use the thumbs to stretch the leather at head and tail enough to cap the headbands (100). Mould the leather to a flat top, on the headbands, approximately to the thickness of the boards. Use a pointed folder to form an S shape on either side of the headbands at the joints (101). Tap and manipulate the head and tail with a folder until the spine is an even rectangular shape (102). Remove excess paste and finger marks with a damp sponge and finally set the groove by running a bone folder along it as before. Place between clean paper in boards with their edges up to the string and leave overnight to dry with a weight on top (not in the press).

Remove the string and ease the stiffness out of the binding. (This operation is known as 'opening' the book.) Open the boards slightly and then shut them. Open and shut them to progressively wider arcs until they swing freely. Then, with the book open on the bench, press down on the boards, let one or two sections drop on either side, press these down and gradually work through the book to the centre (103).

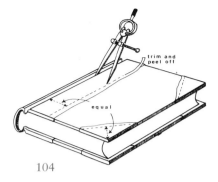

trim and
peel off

equal

104

Mark the leather with dividers as in 104, so that the diagonal bisecting line of each of the corners equals the width of the leather on the sides, and trim away the uneven leather on the outside with a knife and straight-edge, but only as far as the bevelled edge of the boards.

Cut buckram sides, with a turn-in of 18mm, and wide enough to overlap the leather by 1mm. If using corners, cut to shape as in 69, and glue them on as in Project 3. Trim out the leather and buckram together on the inside of the boards. Fill in with manilla, and sandpaper the bumps caused by the inserted flange. Paste down the endpapers 'shut' as in Project 6. Press the book overnight until dry.

Project 8 Limp binding in whole morocco or rexine

Rounded only

Yapp edges (i.e. the leather or rexine overlaps the edges of the pages, covering them completely for protection)

Tipped on endpapers

Registers (page markers)

Materials

One Bible, prayer book or book of poetry

Other materials and equipment as in Project 7, plus:
   two lengths of 5mm silk or nylon ribbon for the registers
   pieces of white nylon or silk for the headbands
   rexine for the cover, if required
   brown paper

Poetry and devotional books are traditionally bound in the limp style (i.e. with soft covers). They have larger squares than usual, some have Yapp edges, and the corners are rounded to wear better. Such bindings are attractive, pleasant to handle and light to carry.

Method

Prepare the book as follows. Remove the old covers and endpapers, without damaging the sewing or tapes if any. Clean the spine by smothering it with paste. After five minutes' soaking, carefully scrape away the softened glue and linings. Repair any damage, as on pp.33-34. If the sewing is found to have broken down, collate and pull the book, knock out the old groove as in Project 5 and press the book for one week.

Resew the sections if necessary (Bibles and prayer books are usually strongly sewn, so may not need resewing). Small books should be sewn in the French style (without tapes; 35E), but larger ones with three or four thin tapes (see pp.35-36). As this type of book is not backed, some extra swell is needed to retain the shape of the spine, but if it is really excessive do not sew every section all along, but sew the first and last six sections all along and the rest two up, as on p.38. As the

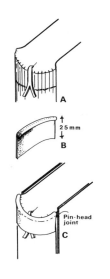

105

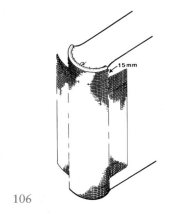

106

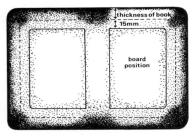

107

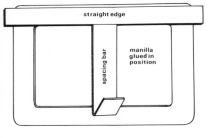

108

edges should not be cut (because the margins are likely to be narrow), it is important to ensure that the sections are kept level during sewing.

Prepare the endpapers as on p.31 (27A). Traditionally, devotional books have black endpapers, but there is no other reason why this should be so, so the colour is left to the discrimination of the binder.

Tip the endpapers in position. Follow the instructions for rounding on p.44, manipulating the sections by hand or by shaping them with a cutting board. Do not use a hammer, as it may damage the flimsy paper. Hold the sections in a symmetrical round shape between two pieces of scrapboard and screw them into the finishing press to protect them. Rub thin glue between the sections and leave the book in the press until it is dry.

Page markers ('registers') are narrow ribbons about 50mm longer than the book. Split the ribbons in half lengthwise for 25mm, glue the halves to the spine at the head, and tuck the ends between the sections (105A). Sew narrow headbands (pp.48-49), or stick on simple headbands of thin string covered with white silk (105B). Covers are of manilla card cut 2mm less at the spine (to allow for the 'pin-head' joint 105C) and extend over the head, tail and foredge for 2mm as squares. Round off the corners of the manilla so that they run parallel to those of the sections. Glue the spine, place the first lining into position, so that it supports the headband and extends freely on either side for 30mm. Trim it as in 106. Apply the second lining, if used, as in Project 4. (This is often omitted, as the spine should be flexible; however, it is an advantage in heavier books.)

Place the book accurately between its manilla boards so that a template for the covering can be made, as follows. Cut a piece of waste paper the size of the book plus 15mm for the turn-in, plus the thickness of the book less 1mm (107). Wrap the paper round the book and mark off the required margins. Cut the leather or rexine from the template and round off the corners. Pare the leather as illustrated in 107, making it extra thin at the corners. Leather will distort during paring, so compare it with the template and recut if necessary.

Measure the width of the spine on a piece of paper and add 4mm for the pin-head joints. Cut a piece of card to this width, for use as a spacing bar. Lay the cover out, with a straight-edge across the top, and mark the width of the overlap with a biro or Conté crayon (108). Place the spacing bar in the centre. Apply glue to both manilla boards and position them on the leather so that they touch both the bar and the straight-edge. Remove both aids, rub the manilla down and leave the cover to dry. Draw a line on the leather or rexine, half the thickness of the book less one millimetre from the edges of the

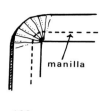

109

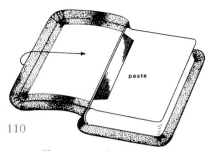

110

Order of operations

1 Prepare book (collate and pull if necessary)
2 Clean off back and repair if necessary
3 Press if required
4 Make endpapers
5 Mark up for sewing if necessary
6 Sew if necessary
7 Tip on endpapers
8 Round
9 Glue spine
10 Attach registers and headbands
11 Cut manilla boards
12 Apply first (and second) linings
13 Make template for cover
14 Cut leather or rexine and pare leather
15 Cut spacing bar
16 Make case
17 Trim the inside
18 Finish if required
19 Attach spine to cover
20 Put down endpapers
21 Form the overlap

manilla. Paste the leather (or glue the rexine) and turn it in on these lines to provide the Yapp. Rub the edges firmly and push any wrinkles out of the leather. Paste (or glue) the corners well, then trim and pleat them into a neat fan shape by manipulating the folds of the material with a thin folder (109). Tap the corners with a light hammer to firm them down. Wash off excess adhesive. Leave the cover to dry between pressing boards, but not in the press.

When dry, pare off overlapping layers at the corners and trim out carefully, taking care not to cut into the manilla. Paring and trimming will be concealed by the endpapers.

The case should now be titled and decorated if appropriate, as finishing can be problematic with the book in place; see Project 8a.

All limp bindings should have tight backs, so proceed as follows. Paste (or for rexine, glue) the back of the cover and glue the spine of the book. Position the book between the manilla boards, maintaining the 2mm pin-head joints and the 2mm squares, and rub the back firmly with a folder, shielding the cover with scrap leather so that it is not bruised. Leave to dry under a weight.

Put down endpapers as follows. Place a waste sheet under the board paper and apply paste to the mull (jaconette or tapes) and paper, remove the waste and shut the cover onto the board paper (110). Repeat for the other side and rub both down well. Open the cover just enough to slip in wax paper as a moisture barrier. Cut two pieces of brown paper, one the width of the manilla boards and over twice the length, and the other the length of the boards and over twice the width. Wrap these very tightly around the book and fix them in position with adhesive tape to 'form' the overlap (111). Leave the book thus for some hours.

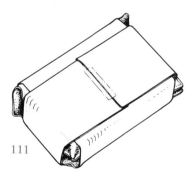

111

Project 9 Loose-leaf photograph
   album in whole cloth (*or*
   quarter or half binding)
Landscape format, to take two
   90 x 112mm photographs side
   by side
Guarded (i.e. with narrow strips
   of paper, 'compensating
   guards', which make up for
   the later addition of
   photographs)
Corded

Materials

Twelve sheets of coloured manilla or equivalent paper,
   each 140 × 316mm
Twelve strips of the same paper for the guards, each 25
   × 140mm
Three pieces of 1800 gsm strawboard, 152 × 322mm,
   152 × 25mm and 152 × 291mm
Two pieces of bookcloth, 192 × 362mm and 192 ×
   396mm (*or* enough for a quarter or half binding, plus
   decorated paper)
Two sheets of coloured Ingres paper, 140 × 310mm and
   140 × 278mm
One piece of coloured lacing cord, 3mm diameter,
   650mm long
Manilla for filling in

This project requires accurate measuring in millimetres.

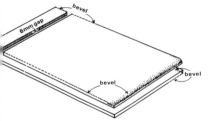

112. Boards with one edge
   bevelled, the others yet to be
   done

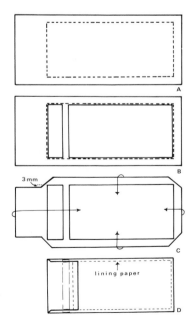

113

Method

Study the description of loose-leaf bindings on p.23.
Place the largest piece of strawboard on the bench, and
on top of it place the smallest one so that it aligns to the
left, and the medium one so that it aligns to the right.
The 6mm gap between the top two boards will be the
hinge. Bevel the outside edges of the three boards with
sandpaper (112). Position the largest strawboard in the
centre of the smaller piece of bookcloth, draw a pitch
line on the bookcloth round the edges of the board and
remove it. Glue the cloth; return the board within the
pitch lines, cut off the corners of the cloth and turn it in.
Rub down, shaping the cloth to the bevelled edges. Place
this covered board on the other piece of cloth to the
right, 20mm from three edges, and draw pitch lines
around it (113A). Remove the board and glue the cloth.
Align the two smaller boards to the pitch marks (B). Cut
the cloth as in (C). Turn it in and rub it down, sealing
the cloth against the hinge gap on both sides (D). Both
covered boards will now be the same size, the upper
with a 6mm hinge reinforced with the extra turn-in.
Trim the turn-in if it is uneven and fill in with manilla on
both boards, as in 91. Paste the two coloured papers to
line the boards, the larger piece to the lower board (D).
Leave under a weight to dry.
   Mark one of the narrow strips of manilla with two
crosses, 30mm from the top and bottom, placed
centrally. Using the crosses as centres, punch two holes
5mm in diameter. With this template make holes in the
other strips and also in the sheets, always aligning the
template against the left-hand side. Centre the template

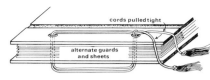

114

Order of operations

1 Cut all materials
2 Bevel edges of boards
3 Cover base board
4 Cover hinged board
5 Trim inside
6 Fill in
7 Paste down linings
8 Leave to dry
9 Make template for punching holes
10 Punch holes
11 Eyelet
12 Score paper if necessary
13 Assemble

against the left-hand edge of the hinged board and cut holes. Align the hinged board exactly with the other one, ring the position of the holes with a pencil and make the holes. The punch may cause an eruption on the board, and this should be flattened with a hammer. Insert the eyelets.

If the sheets do not bend easily, place a straight-edge 25mm from the left of each sheet and score the paper with a thin bone folder. Move the straight-edge 2mm to the right and score again. Six creases should be adequate.

Assemble the album, so that the sheets and guards fall alternately, and tie it together with the coloured lacing cord (114). Tie a knot 25mm from each end of the cord and fray the threads to make a tassel. Pages can then be removed and others added, and the whole is tightened by pulling the cord.

This loose-leaf album can also be quarter or half bound, but as this is a landscape format the strips and corner diagonals should be less than a quarter of the total width. The exact measurement is left to the binder's discrimination.

Project 10 Enclosed slip case

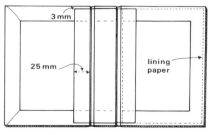

115

Materials

1800 gsm strawboard for the outer case
1400 gsm strawboard for the inner case
Coloured Ingres paper for linings
Bookcloth for covering
Instant glue
Manilla for filling in

This is an introduction to box making, and its principles are the same for the most complicated of work. Accuracy in measuring, cutting board and the skilful use of materials and adhesives are essential. Boxes must be strongly constructed to protect their contents. Unlike books they are easily replaced, so inorganic glue, impervious to moisture, may be used (see pp.21, 22). The pH value of all materials should be as near neutral as possible so that the contents are unaffected (see p.13). The more common slip case, which leaves the spine uncovered, is unsatisfactory, as the spine is vulnerable to mishandling, dust and the fading effects of light. The enclosed slip case is therefore recommended. It will be easier if one begins with a box for a thick book.

Method

The inner case (115). For the sides, cut two pieces of 1400 gsm strawboard the height of the book plus 2mm

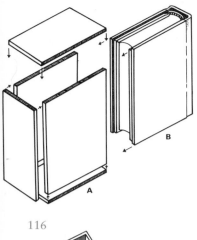

116

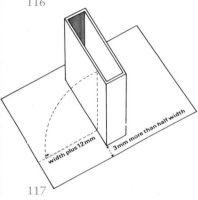

117

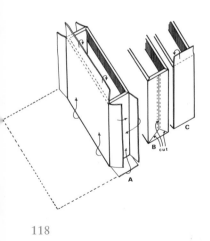

118

and the width of the book less 4mm. For the spine, cut a strip of strawboard the same board length and as wide as the book plus 2mm. With these, make a case in whole cloth, as in Project 4. Reinforce the spine with a strip of cloth as in 115. Trim the inside, fill in with manilla and line with pasted coloured paper within 3mm of the edges. Leave the case to dry.

The outer case (116A). Place the book in the inner case and cut two 1800 gsm strawboards 1mm larger than the inner case all round and place these on either side of the case. Pinch the book, case and boards together with finger and thumb. Release the pressure slowly until expansion stops. Mark the distance between the outside edges of the boards, plus 1mm, on a piece of paper. Cut the spine of the slip case to this width and to the height of the side boards. Also cut top and bottom pieces to this width, and as wide as the side board plus the thickness of the board (116A). Line the five boards with the same coloured paper as used on the case, as follows. Cut the papers larger by about 12mm, paste them, rub them down onto the boards and, before they are dry, sandpaper the excess away. Before the drying paper begins to warp the boards, assemble the box, joining the edges with instant glue. Support the pieces with pressing boards and scrap card until dry. Sandpaper any discrepancies at the joins.

Make a template and cut the cloth as in 117. Cover as illustrated in 118. First draw a pitch line in the centre of the cloth. Glue the spine of the box, place it centrally on this line and rub down. Cut the cloth as in 118A. Glue one side of the box at a time. Pull the cloth onto the sides, cut as illustrated and turn the overlap into the inside. Glue the cloth flaps and turn them in onto the sides. Use a scalpel to cut through both pieces of cloth through the centre and diagonals at the ends (118B). Lift the cloth, peel away the excess and rub down so that all the edges fit neatly together. Trim away extra cloth along the open edges. Cover the top and bottom with strips of glued cloth to the same width and 12mm longer (118C). Turn the overlap into the inside. On the inside of the box, cover the cloth overlap within 3mm of the edges by 50mm-wide strips of the same coloured paper as used previously. Use paste rather than glue so that the strips may be manoeuvred into position. Leave to dry. Place the book and inner case into the slipcase. With normal hand pressure on the sides, the book should not fall out even if turned upside down. Ease the pressure, and the book and case should slide gently from the box. (Finger-holds cut in the sides are not necessary. Should the book be too loose, line the boards on the inside of the slip case with more coloured paper 50mm wide.)

Finishing

Project 1a Single-section
pamphlet binding

Initials tooled with gold foil

Materials

Several sheets of bank paper, for practice
One alphabet of hand letters, 16pt size
Scrap bookcloth and card, for practice
Gold foil
Cooling pad

Method

Tool two or three initials on the cloth with foil,
following the instructions on pp. 54-55.

Project 2a Single-section
pamphlet binding

Initials and decoration tooled
with gold foil

Materials

As for Project 1a, plus decorative hand tools and pallets.

Method

Tool initials on the front board, as for Project 1a, then
decorate the rest of the cover (paper and cloth) with
decorative hand tools, to your own design. (Practise first
on paper.)

Project 3a Single-section
pamphlet binding

Title tooled with gold foil on
front board cloth or across the
decorated paper

Materials

As for Project 1a.
This project concentrates on correct letter spacing.

Method

Impress the chosen letters onto bank paper as before,
but pay particular attention to the spacing. Both
'automatic' spacing (the same distance between each
letter, as in 119a) and equal areas between letters (119B)
result, paradoxically, in an uneven appearance. Try to
position the letters so that the 'weight' of the spaces
(distance *and* area) is equal, taking into account the
shape of each letter (119c). If possible, keep letters well
apart rather than crowded together. If placed vertically,
the title may read from top to bottom or vice versa, but
letters placed vertically, one under the other, tend to
make words illegible. Tool the letters as before, striking
recurring letters consecutively, although a longer dwell
may be necessary as the tool loses heat.

119

Project 4a Multi-section address
book

Title tooled with gold foil on
front board and spine

Index lettered in gold

Materials

As for Project 1a, plus one piece of millboard to place
under each tab while tooling.

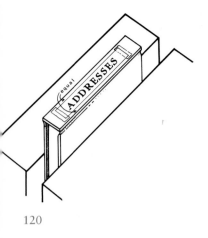

120

Method

Front board. Letter the word 'ADDRESSES' on paper and tape the template centrally, a third of the way down, before tooling as before.

Spine. If required, letter as follows. (It is preferable aesthetically to position the title towards the head of the book. It can be placed in the centre, but should then be centred optically by moving it 3mm towards the head.) To facilitate placing the title on the spine with equal space above and below it, make a template as in 120, but cut it out with an equal margin above and below the letters, so that the combined width is slightly less than that of the spine. The template may then be placed without difficulty dead in the centre, simply by judging the distance on either side of it.

Index. Place a piece of millboard under the first leaf of each initial before lettering it. Hold the foil level with the bottom of the tab and impress each letter direct without paper templates. Do not use hard pressure or the paper will buckle.

Project 5a Multi-section binding

Long title tooled with gold foil on spine and front board, with border

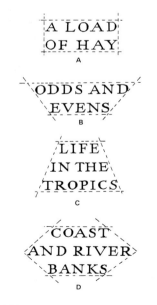

121

Materials

As the spine is hollow, a thin strip of hard but flexible plastic or metal to make a firm base for tooling

One piece of cloth mounted on a piece of wood similar in shape to the spine of the book, for practice

One strip of manilla

Single-line pallet

Decorative pallet

Method

The cases of backed books are best lettered before the sections are pasted in, so that one can work on the spine while it is flat. Otherwise, for a hollow spine, a thin strip of hard but flexible plastic or metal can be inserted to make a firm base on which to tool. Before attempting the actual binding, practise on cloth mounted on a similar-shaped piece of wood.

Spine. It is preferable to letter across the spine, but if the words are long and the spine narrow, they should be placed vertically and can read up or down. The lines of lettering should not exceed the 'readable width', which is 3mm within each side of the spine. Letters will thus not become foreshortened by the curve. Decide on the best 'shape' for the title, as in 121. (This is normally a triangle, pyramid, lozenge or rectangle.) Small words should not have lines to themselves, but should be included in lines above or below, as appropriate to the sense. If space allows, use 'AND' rather than an ampersand. Do not shorten words, and split them only

83

if really necessary; this should be done at the phonetic divisions and a hyphen used. Titles may be shortened: for example, 'A BOOK OF ENGLISH VERSE' might be abbreviated to 'ENGLISH VERSE'. Decide on the point size of the letters, according to the arrangement of the words, their length, and the width of the spine.

Make the template as follows. Measure the height of the chosen letters with dividers and prick off a number of these distances beneath each other on bank paper. Use the blunt end of the dividers to draw a defined line between every other mark. These will provide guide lines for the words with equal spaces between. Ensure that the spelling follows that of the title page. Letter the longest line on the paper first, paying due attention to the spacing of letters and words (see Project 3a). Check that it will fit across the spine. Then draw two parallel lines on either side of it and a line down the middle (122). The middle letter of the top line, in this case 'A', should be placed on the centre line, with 'CO' and 'ST' on either side. Follow this procedure for the bottom line. This will ensure that the title is symmetrical. Cut the template out with an equal margin to the left and right of the letters, as in Project 4a. Attach the template to the spine, place gold foil underneath and tool as before.

With practice, it is possible to work without the template, directly on the foil, as follows: draw lines on the foil for the words and the spaces in between with a sharp pencil before taping the foil to the spine. Indicate the centre of each line by touching the foil with one point of a pair of dividers, and letter from the middle outwards, to left and right. The letters must obviously be positioned accurately, as there is no opportunity for correction afterwards.

Tool gold lines around the title as follows. Set the book in the finishing press with the spine running across you from left to right. Estimate the positions of the lines: the space between the top line and the top row of letters should be a little more than the height of the letters, and the space between the bottom row of letters and the bottom line more than that at the top. Hold a piece of foil in position, with a strip of manilla over it so that the edge of the foil shows where the line is required (123). Heat the pallet and hold it firmly in the fist. Bend over the work, keeping the elbow well out from the body. First position the pallet by its straight side over the work, then place one end against the manilla and, using this as a guide, press firmly across the spine, always keeping the tool at right angles to the spine. (A decorative pallet is used in the same way.)

Front board. Make a template for the lettering on the front board in the same way, adjusting the spacing and point size to suit the size of the cover, and tool as for the spine.

122

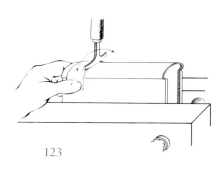

123

Project 6a Library-style binding in whole buckram

Title and border tooled with gold leaf on a leather label

Materials

As on pp.52-53, plus enough morocco for the label.

Method

Although it is possible to tool directly on the buckram with gold foil, a label is used here to introduce tooling with gold leaf. Lay out the title on bank paper as in Project 5a, to determine the size of the leather label, and allowing for the top and bottom spaces. Pare a piece of leather larger than this, very thinly, and from it cut out the label. Pare the edges at an angle of 45 degrees, as on p.50, paste the label to the spine and leave it to dry. Follow the instructions for gold leaf tooling (Method 1) on p.55. Tool a line around the edge of the panel, or ornament it with a decorative pallet, as in Project 5a.

Alternatively, the pared piece of leather can be taped to a piece of millboard, tooled and then cut to size before being pasted onto the spine. This method is, however, not always successful, as the tooling is often disturbed when the label is pasted and rubbed down.

Project 7a Library-style binding in half leather

Title and cataloguing information tooled on spine with gold leaf (*or* personally designed spines and sides tooled in blind or with gold leaf on leather, and with gold foil on cloth)

124

Materials

As on pp.52-53.

Method 1: the conventional library style

The finishing should always show information for reference and storage, so the title, author, volume number and date if appropriate, and the name of the library and press mark (catalogue coding) should be tooled on the spine (124). The sides are left plain.

Spine. This should be divided into six panels by gold or blind lines (see p.57). Work out the divisions and mark the ends of the lines on the leather with a touch from a pair of dividers. Join the points with a strip of manilla as in 123, and mark the lines clearly with the finishing (smaller) bone folder or heated pallet. Lay out on bank paper the title, the information required and decoration if any, attach this template to the leather and blind tool (see p.55). Prepare the leather for gold tooling with the paste wash and glaire and apply the gold leaf with vaseline as on pp.55-56. Tool both letters and decoration. Heat the pallet and use the folder marks or blind impressions to guide the tool across the spine.

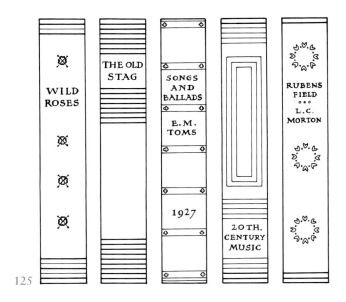

125

Method 2: personally designed bindings

Design the entire binding full size on bond paper, using pencil lines for the pallet and fillet lines and actual impressions from the tools for letters and decoration (125, 126). Attach this paper template to the cover with adhesive tape. (Do not press adhesive tape onto paper, as it will leave an unsightly mark.) Blind tool the lettering and decoration onto the leather only, through the paper pattern. At the same time, tool any decoration on the cloth by placing foil under the template and tooling with decorative hand tools. Mark the beginnings and ends of pallet and fillet lines with a light touch of the dividers on the spine and sides, as for the conventional library style. Remove the template. Complete the lines across the spine with a single or double pallet in

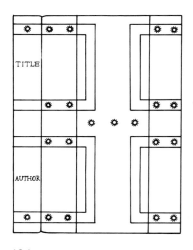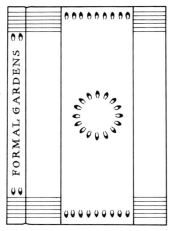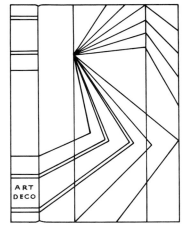

126

blind tooling, using a strip of manilla to link the two ends as a guide. Those on the leather on the front board, whether to be left blind or gilded, are put in from the beginnings to the ends, with the finishing folder. It will facilitate the accurate gold tooling of lines of decoration to be done with a decorative pallet, if a pallet line is tooled in blind across the spine as a guide. Tool all these lines, letters and decoration on the leather in gold leaf, or leave some blind, according to the original design, following the instructions on pp.55-56. When tooling gold lines near light-coloured cloth or paper, which is liable to staining when the vaseline is applied, it is advisable to apply a light coat of vaseline to the face of the heated tool and pick up the gold from the gold cushion with this, rather than vaselining the leather itself and using cotton wool.

Pallet and fillet lines in gold on cloth

Draw light pencil lines on foil and cut the foil into lengths corresponding to those of the lines required. Position the foil on the cloth, so that the pencil lines touch the beginning and end points of the lines already marked on the cloth with dividers. Tape the foil firmly in position and tool with the heated pallet or fillet, guided by the pencil lines (127). Remember to start and finish fillet lines with a matching small pallet, or a mitred fillet (128).

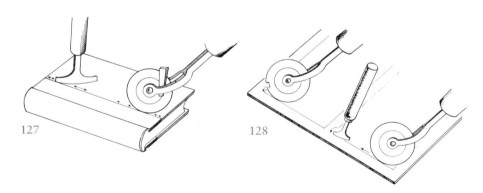

127

128

Glossary

adhesive binding, unsewn binding. A binding made of single sheets stuck together with glue or paste. The adhesive is applied either to the extreme back margins or to the roughened edges of the knocked-up sheets. See also sewn binding.

all along. A method of sewing in which one or more sections are sewn along their length (34). See also two up, three up.

antique paper. A rough, uncalendered paper; it is light in weight, with bulk, but little size.

A0. The basic size in the ISO (International Standards Organization) series of papers and boards, 1189 × 841 mm (i.e. one square metre).

art paper, coated paper. A paper usually made from esparto grass fibre, coated with china clay and casein glue and glazed with rollers under pressure. Used for fine screen printing.

back. The spine of a book.

back fold. The inner margin of folded sections. Sometimes referred to as the binding margin, as it is where the sections are secured by stitching (34).

backing. Providing a joint to the spine (43C).

backing boards. Wedge-shaped boards, usually of beech. They are angled at the wide ends to assist in making the joint on the spine when backing (48).

bank. A thin writing paper, white or tinted. See also bond.

bead. An embroidery thread crossing over at the base of the headbanding core, to create a raised, bead-like effect (53F).

bevelled boards. Covering boards which are thinned down at an angle at the edges to present a more elegant appearance.

binding. A bookcover, in any style.

blanket stitching. A method of sewing in which the thread pierces the side of the sections and is then looped around the back edges of them (35D).

blind tooling. Making a dark impression in leather, by impressing either a hot finishing tool into it, or a cold tool that has first been dabbed in printer's ink.

blinding in. Making an impression in leather or cloth with a heated finishing tool, as a guide for gold tooling (see p.55).

board paper. See endpapers.

bolt. The folds which occur at head and foredge when a sheet is folded into a section.

bond. A heavier substance of writing paper than bank.

bookcloth. Economical book-covering material, made from woven cotton.

buckram. Stong and expensive book-covering material, made from woven linen or a mixture of linen and cotton.

calendered paper. Paper polished to a high glaze by pressure or friction from calendering rollers.

cartridge paper. Hard, tough, opaque, uncoated paper used for drawing and printing. Also suitable for endpapers.

case. An economical form of binding. The front and back boards, together with the covering material to which they are stuck, form a cover for the sewn sections, which are pasted inside (77).

case binding, (publisher's) edition binding. A mass-produced, machine-bound book, with a case rather than a cover. It is not a true binding style, but can nevertheless be imitated by the craft binder.

case making. The operation, done by hand, of joining two boards together with the covering material to make a case.

catch stitch. Synonym of kettle stitch.

cerf, kerf. A slot or cutting sawn into the backs of the sections at head and tail, in which the kettle stitch is made (34).

chemical wood paper. Paper which is made from fibres left after other acidic parts of the wood have been dissolved away by caustic sodas. The most commonly used paper in craft bookbinding. See also mechanical wood paper.

collate. To check a book thoroughly to ensure that it is complete and in the right order.

coated paper. Synonym of art paper.

colophon. 1. In old books, an inscription at the beginning or end of a book, often including the printer's name and details of production. 2. In modern books, the publisher's device.

covering. The operation of covering a binding in cloth, leather, vellum or other material.

cut flush. With the cover cut flush with, i.e. the same size as, the sections.

cutting boards. Wedge-shaped boards, usually of beech, right-angled at the wide ends and used when cutting the edges of books (38).

cutting pad, cutting wedge. A pile of paper placed against the sewn sections in the lying press while cutting the head and tail, to compensate for the swell (73).

deckle edge. The conspicuous broken edge on handmade paper, caused by the fibres creeping between the deckle frame and the sieve during manufacture (see p.17).

double sewing. Sewing one or more sections of a book twice, particularly when the thread is doubled round the tapes (e.g. in the exposed cloth-jointed endpaper), to reinforce the binding (35H).

dwell. The time for which the hot tool is impressed in the leather while gold or blind tooling.

edge gilding. The application of gold leaf to the edges of the leaves of a book. Edge gilding is not discussed in this book, as it is only for the advanced worker.

edge pare. The paring away of the edge of a piece of leather at an angle of 45 degrees (54,55).

edition binding. Synonym of

case binding.

embossed. (Paper, cloth, leather, etc.) Impressed with a pattern or false grain.

endpapers. The sheets of paper (two or more) which come between the cover and the sewn sections. Part of the binding construction, they comprise, at their most basic, a board paper (which is usually coloured and which serves to counteract the warp of the boards caused by the covering material) and a free fly leaf, which protects the first or last pages of text. (See Chapter 5.)

engine sizing. In the production of paper, the addition of resin size to the pulp at the mixer stage, before it is made into paper (see p.18).

filler. A chemical such as china clay, starch, etc., added to paper and cloth to bulk it out. When added to paper it also makes it whiter and more receptive to high polishing for fine printing. See also filling in.

filling in. The operation of filling in the space on the inside of the front or back board left uncovered by the cloth, etc., with pulp or manilla card. This levels the surfaces so that the endpapers lie flat (91) and is called a filler.

finishing. The second of two principal processes involved in binding a book: the titling, decoration and polishing of the cover. See also forwarding.

flexible style. A style of binding in which the sections are sewn onto lengths of twisted pigskin or hemp cord (known as bands) placed across and on the outside of the sections. The ends of these are called slips and are laced into the boards. The binding has a tight back.

flush binding. A binding whose cover is the same size as the sections.

fly leaf. See endpapers.

fold to paper. Folding sections by machine (and occasionally by hand) by lining up the edges of the paper.

fold to print. When the printed type is out of square with the edge of the sheet, lining up the top line of type at each fold so that the margins are even. This applies only to hand folding.

folio. 1. A sheet of paper in one of the traditional sizes, folded once to give two leaves. 2. A book made of such sheets, i.e. the largest format possible in that particular size (see p.19).

foredge. The front edge of a book, opposite the spine (17). So called because this edge originally faced outward from the shelves and the title was painted, inked or scorched on the edges of the leaves.

forwarding. The first of the two principal processes involved in bookbinding: the production of the binding itself. See also finishing.

French groove. In the library style, the groove down the edge of the spine, between the joint and the board (80). Its function is to enable the thick leather used in this binding style to fold more easily at the hinge.

French sewing. The sewing together of two or more sections without tapes. Each section is linked to the rest by catching up the loops of thread of the preceding section (35E).

frontispiece. The illustration facing the title page of a book.

full binding. Synonym of whole binding.

gathering. Collecting the sections or sheets together in the correct sequence to make up a complete book.

glaire, glair. A preparation of white of egg or shellac used to fix the gold leaf in tooling and edge gilding.

gold foil. Gold (or gold substitute) sprayed electronically onto a plastic, paper or cellophane backing. Used industrially for the titling of mass-produced books and by the craft binder for economical bindings.

gold leaf. An alloy of 22 carats gold and 2 carats silver, beaten by machine to a thinness of 1/250,000 of an inch. (.0000025 cm) and used for titling and decorating books.

grain (direction), machine direction. The orientation of the fibres in paper and board (see p.18), or of the warp thread in cloth. The grain must always run from head to tail of the book.

gsm. Grams per square metre. The standard measurement now used for weighing paper and board.

guard book. A type of binding, e.g. a photograph album, in which the spine is bulked out by the addition of narrow strips or folds of paper so that it is the right size when photographs, etc., are added (114).

guards, guarding. 1. Strips of paper or cloth pasted or glued to the back folds of sections, or to single diagrams, maps, etc., for their repair or reinforcement. 2. Narrow folds or strips of paper or card used in guard books (114).

half binding. An economy covering style in which the spine and corners, or spine and foredge strips, are covered with a good material (e.g. leather) and the remainder with a cheaper one (e.g. cloth) (24).

half title page. The recto of the first or second leaf of a book, on which is printed the brief title.

head. The top edge of a binding or page (17).

headband. A true headband consists of coloured threads entwined tightly round a core of vellum backed with leather, and is sewn through the sections (17, 53G), filling the gap at the spine between the top or bottom of the section and the edges of the boards. It thus helps to prevent the sections collapsing through the effect of gravity, and also serves to lessen the damage done when the book is pulled off the shelf by its headcap. Imitation headbands, which are purely decorative, are merely stuck to the back folds of the sections.

headcap. In leather bindings, a shaped and modelled turn-in over the top and bottom of the spine (17).

hollow. A paper tube stuck to the spine of a book, to which the covering material is attached. The resulting hollow back allows a freer opening for sections of stiff paper, or for books in which entries are to be made, and allows books bound in stiff material such as vellum and buckram to open more freely (51).

hot pressed. Paper which is glazed (rather than surfaced) by being pressed when dry between hot, polished metal plates. Used for writing and fine printing paper. See also 'not' and 'rough'.

imposition. The arrangement of each page of type and illustrations so that they are in the correct sequence when the sheet is printed and folded (see p.23; 20).

insert. Additional matter placed within a book or pamphlet without being permanently fixed (e.g. a diagram in a pocket at the end of a book).

inset. (To fix) additional matter within a book by sewing or sticking, e.g. an illustration plate within the text.

jaconette. White cotton cloth, open or closely woven according to quality, which is stiffened with a starch filler to facilitate handling and prevent the penetration of glue. Used for strengthening sections, maps, endpapers, spines and the hinges of books.

jog. US term for knock up.

joint, shoulder. The right-angled groove formed in the back folds of the sections, in which the boards are placed (43C).

kerf. See cerf.

kettle stitch, catch stitch. A catch stitch or knot made at the end of each section to join it to the preceding one (34). (From the German word *ketteln*, 'to pick up stitches'.)

knock up (US: jog). To tap the sections or sheets at the spine and head so that they lie evenly and squarely. It is an important part of many binding operations, especially before cutting the edges (46).

kraft. A strong, brown wrapping paper used as a second lining to reinforce the spine of a book (80). It is also used for making the hollow.

laid (paper). Handmade paper showing parallel wire marks about 25 mm apart in one direction, with close-set wire marks in the other. These marks are caused by the sieve operated by the paper maker (see p.17). The pattern can be imitated on machine-made papers by means of the Dandy roller (see p.18)

laminated. (Used of two or more materials.) Stuck together in layers.

leather cloth. Synonym of rexine.

library style. A utility binding developed around the beginning of the twentieth century, when the public library system became widespread. It incorporated innovations and structural differences that give strength and durability, such as sewn-on tapes, reinforced endpapers and a thick leather cover (80). It normally has a tight back, and its main feature is the French groove (81B).

limp binding. A soft cover, very often with both squares extending over half the thickness of the book, thus enclosing the edges of the pages. Bibles are often limp bound.

linings. 1. Pieces of strong paper pasted to the inside of boards to prevent their being warped by the covering material. 2. The two pieces of material which are used to strengthen the spine, the first being of mull and the second of kraft (80).

loaded stick. A piece of wood $250 \times 25 \times 25$ mm, with a piece of lead attached to one end and bound with leather. It is used to beat the swell in the backs of sections while sewing, to reduce it.

loading. In paper making, the addition of kaolin or similar substances to the pulp at the mixer stage, to give opacity and a receptive surface for printing (see p.18).

loose-leaf binding. A binding made up of single sheets of paper or other material, with or without holes punched or slots cut in the back margins, and held together by thongs, cords, posts, rings, wire spirals, plastic combs, bars or spring mechanisms (18).

machine-finished paper (m/f). Paper as it leaves the machine without further surface treatment.

made (Used of endpapers, etc.) With two or more pieces of paper or board laminated with an adhesive (27D).

marbled paper. Paper with a decorative, marble-like appearance, obtained by laying it onto a viscous liquid so that it picks up colours floating on the surface (see p.28).

mechanical wood paper. Wood (usually spruce) which is ground to pulp by machine and then made into paper. As it contains many impurities, it soon deteriorates and is used only for ephemeral printing.

morocco. Fine leather made from goatskin, and tanned with oak bark or sumach.

mould-made paper. Paper made on a machine in separate sheets. It is usually of good quality.

mull, super. An open-weave cotton cloth stiffened with starch to facilitate handling. It is used as the first lining on the spine (80).

nick. A groove cut in the shank of a decorative finishing tool, handle letter (or type) to assist in accurate placing (63).

'not' (not glazed). Handmade paper with a slightly uneven surface imparted to it by being pressed when wet between fine felt mats, or 'blankets' (see p.17). Used in fine printing and drawing.

octavo. A sheet of paper of any traditional size, folded three times to make a section of eight leaves (see p.19).

old groove. The groove remaining in the back edges of the folded sections after a book has been taken apart. This must be flattened or 'knocked out' with a hammer before rebinding (76).

onlay. A method of decorating a book bound in leather by pasting pieces of leather, often of different colours, directly onto the leather cover, and tooling the edges to bind them down. (See *The Thames and Hudson Manual of Bookbinding*, pp.206-10.)

opening a book. Easing the stiffness out of a newly bound book (see p.75; 103).

overcasting, oversewing. Reinforcing a section, or joining a number of single sheets together, by sewing through the back margin (35F).

overhang. Synonym of squares.

overlap. Synonym of turn-in.

PIRA test. A test of bookbinding leathers to ascertain that they are free from injurious acids. It was instigated by the Printing Industries Research Association, and leather which has passed this test should bear the letters PIRA.

pitch lines, pitch marks. Lines or marks drawn on one material to assist in positioning another material onto it quickly and accurately, especially when glue is used (72).

plates. Diagrams and illustrations printed on different paper from the text and bound either with the text or as separate leaves or sections (see p.25).

'prelims', preliminaries, preliminary matter. The preliminary pages of a book, comprising the half-title page, the frontispiece, the title page, the imprint page, the contents page and any other pages up to the beginning of the main text. They often form the first section. In old books these pages are usually numbered with Roman numerals. (See p.24).

protection sheet. Synonym of waste sheet.

pulling. Freeing the sections of a book from the original binding, in preparation for rebinding (see p.68).

quarter binding. An economical covering method in which one piece of good material (e.g. leather) is used to cover the spine, extending over part of the sides as well, and a cheaper one to cover the remainder (24). The effect can be pleasing if the materials are of a high quality.

quarto. A sheet of paper folded twice to make four leaves (see p.19).

quire. A quantity of paper: 24 sheets of handmade, 25 sheets of machine made.

ream. A quantity of paper: 480 sheets of handmade, 500 sheets of machine made.

recto. The right-hand page of a book, usually with an odd page number.

register. A page-marker made of a length of ribbon, one end of which is glued to the spine before lining (105).

retree. 'Seconds' in handmade paper. These are usually sheets that have some slight blemish.

rexine, leather cloth. Cloth surfaced with a mixture of cellulose nitrate, camphor oil and alcohol, and embossed to look like leather.

'rough'. Handmade paper with a rough surface imparted to it by being pressed when wet between heavy felt mats, or 'blankets'. Artists' watercolour paper is an example.

rounding. Shaping the spine of the sewn sections into a third of a circle (47).

saddle stitching. Securing the leaves of a single section by sewing with thread or inserting wire through the back fold (19).

sans-serif, sanserif (typeface). Unornamented with serifs. (French: 'without serifs'.)

sections. A group of folded sheets, usually comprising 4,8,12,16 or 32 pages, which together make up a complete book.

serif. A small 'finishing' line used to embellish roman forms of printed type or other lettering – as, for example, in the typeface used in this book.

setting the back. Fixing the shape of a book's spine permanently, by first pressing it in good shape and applying a thick layer of paste to the spine. In five minutes the paste is scraped to clean off the old glue and the book left to dry, when the shape of the spine is permanently set (see p.71).

sewn binding. A binding made up of sections sewn together. See also adhesive binding.

shoulders. Synonym of joints.

side stitching. Securing sections or a number of single sheets together by sewing with thread or inserting wire through the back margins (19).

siding. In quarter or half bindings (24), covering the remainder of the exposed boards with cloth or paper after the leather or cloth has been attached.

signature. A printed letter or number usually placed at the bottom of the first page of each folded section to assist in the collation of the book (see pp.24-25).

size. A solution of animal gelatin or resin added to paper to improve its permanence, strength, resistance to moisture, and to make it impervious to the penetration of writing and printing ink (see pp.17, 18). See also engine sizing, tub sizing.

spacing bar, pitching bar. A strip of board used to separate the two boards to a desired measurement when making case bindings; it is removed when the covering material is turned in (108).

split board. A board made up of one piece of millboard and one of strawboard, laminated together save for a slit to contain the flange of tapes and waste sheet. It is one of the constructional features of the library style (80).

squares, overhang. The space between the boards or covers of a book and the sections

(17). Their size is dependent on the size, use and binding style of the book. Although the squares protect the leaves, they should not be too large, for the covers must be supported by the leaves.

stab stitching. Securing a large number of single sheets together by driving metal staples more than half way through the back margins, from both sides (19).

start, stert. The projection at the foredge of one leaf or section beyond the others (30). It is usually caused by poor sewing and very thick sections.

stiffener. In a case binding, a strip of paper or thin card, cut to the width of the spine, placed between the boards and glued onto the covering material to stiffen or strengthen the spine cloth (77).

stiff leaf. One piece of paper attached by adhesive to another to increase its substance and strength. The common made endpaper is an example (27D).

substance. The thickness and weight of paper, expressed in gsm (grams per square metre).

sunk cord style. A style of binding in which the sections are sewn onto lengths of hemp cord that are recessed into the backs of the sections. The ends are called slips and are laced into the boards. The binding may be tight or hollow backed and the spine left smooth or with false bands (see flexible style).

super. Synonym of mull.

surface sizing. Synonym of tub sizing.

swell. The additional thickness in the sewn folds of the sections, caused by the sewing thread and any repair paper (43A).

tail. The bottom of a binding or page (17).

three-up. Sewing three sections at a time, with one length of thread, to reduce swell.

tie-down. One of several loops of thread taken under the kettle stitches at intervals when embroidering a headband (53G). It secures the headband to the book.

tight back. A spine in which the covering material, usually leather, is attached directly to the lined or unlined backs of the sections (51). This is a much more durable method than the hollow back, which consists of a paper tube attached to the cover.

tip on, tip in, tip up. To incorporate a single sheet, plate, endpaper or section into a book by applying a narrow strip of adhesive to its back margin and sticking it to the back edge of a section (22A, 27A).

title page. The recto of the third or fourth leaf of a book, on which is printed the complete title of the book, with other information such as author, volume number, date, patron, publisher's name, and place and date of publication.

tool. To title and decorate a binding by impressing engraved tools into the surface of the covering material. The impression can be in gold (gold foil or leaf), in colour (coloured foil) or 'blind' (a dark or black impression caused either by heat and pressure alone or by using a tool dabbed in printer's ink).

trade binding. Prestige and miscellaneous bookbinding done by commercial firms employing journeymen (qualified binders) and apprentices trained in the craft. Most of the work is done by hand, but some machines are used.

tub sizing, surface sizing. The addition of size to paper after it has been manufactured, by passing it through a bath of animal gelatine size (see p.17).

turn-in, turn-over, overlap. The part of the covering material which is turned in over the edges of the boards to protect them (67C, D). It is a characteristic of all books except for some flush bindings.

two-up. Sewing two sections at a time, with one length of thread, to reduce swell (35A).

unsewn binding. Synonym of adhesive binding.

verso. A left-hand page of a book, usually with an even page number.

warp. In cloth, the threads which run the length of the roll. Sometimes referred to as the grain direction. See also weft.

waste sheet, protection sheet. A protective sheet of paper incorporated in the endpapers and either cut down or removed during binding (27B, D).

weaver's knot. A secure knot for joining thread together (31).

weft. In cloth, the threads which run at right angles to the length of the roll.

whole binding, full binding. A binding that is covered entirely in the same material.

wire part. In papermaking, the moving belt of woven phosphor bronze or nylon on which the pulp falls to make the paper web and which thus determines the grain direction of the fibres (see p.18).

wove (paper). Paper without a pattern of wires, which becomes visible when held to the light (see pp.17, 18).

Yapp binding. A form of binding with squares extended to overlap the exposed edges of the paper and cover them completely (110). Yapp bindings are usually limp, with rounded corners, and are used mainly for devotional books. Named after a bookseller in about 1850.

Schools and societies

Schools

UNITED KINGDOM

London

Camberwell School of Arts and Crafts
Peckham Road
LONDON
SE5 8US
Tel. (01) 703 0987

Central London Adult Education Institute
6 Bolt Court
Fleet Street
LONDON
EC4A 3DY
Tel. (01) 353 4153

Chelsea-Westminster Adult Education Institute
Marlborough School
Draycott Avenue
LONDON
SW3 3AA
Tel. (01) 584 0555

City of London Polytechnic
Sir John Cass School of Art
117 Houndsditch
LONDON
EC3N 2EY
Tel. (01) 283 1030

London College of Printing
Clerkenwell Branch
Back Hill
LONDON
EC1R 5EN
Tel. (01) 278 1726

Morley College
61 Westminster Bridge Road
LONDON
SE1 7HT
Tel. (01) 928 8501

The North

College of Ripon and York St John
College Road
YORK

YO2 3US
Tel. (0765) 2691

York College of Arts and Technology
Tadcaster Road
Dringhouses
YORK
YO2 1UA
Tel. (0904) 704141

The Midlands and Central England

Barnfield College
New Bedford Road
LUTON
Beds
LU3 2AX
Tel. (0582) 507531

Oxford Polytechnic
Headington
OXFORD
OX3 0BP
Tel. (0865) 64777

Wolverhampton Polytechic
Faculty of Art and Design
North Street
WOLVERHAMPTON
WV1 1LY
Tel. (0902) 29911

The South West

School of Printing
Brunel Technical College
Ashley Down
BRISTOL
BS7 9BU
Tel. (0272) 41241

The South East

Brighton Polytechnic
Faculty of Art and Design
Grand Parade
BRIGHTON
Sussex
BN2 2JY
Tel. (0273) 604141

Guildford County College of Technology
Stoke Park
GUILDFORD
Surrey
GU1 1EZ
Tel. (0483) 31251

Reigate School of Art and Design
127 Blackborough Road
REIGATE
Surrey
RH2 7DE
Tel. (0734) 66661

Southampton College of Art
Marsh Lane
SOUTHAMPTON
Hants
SO9 4WU
Tel. (0703) 28182

Twickenham College of Technology
Department of Printing and Graphic Design
Egerton Road
TWICKENHAM
Middlesex
TW2 7SJ
Tel. (01) 892 6656

West Dean College of Crafts
West Dean
CHICHESTER
Sussex
PO18 0QZ
Tel. (024 363) 301
(Short courses throughout the year.)

West Surrey College of Art and Design
Falkner Road
The Hart
FARNHAM
Surrey
GU9 7DS
Tel. (0252) 722441

Further information from:
The Department of Education and Science
Art and Further Education
Elizabeth House
York Road
LONDON
SE1 7PH
Tel. (01) 928 9222

USA

California

Capricornus School of Bookbinding and Restoration
P.O. Box 98

BERKELEY
CA 94701
Tel. (415) 658 7930

University of California
Department of the Arts
10995 Le Conte Avenue
LOS ANGELES
CA 90024
Tel. (213) 825 9413

Connecticut
Bookworks
56 Arbor Street
HARTFORD
CT 06106
Tel. (203) 232 3747

Creative Arts Workshop
80 Audubon Street
NEW HAVEN
CT 06510
Tel. (203) 562 4927

Massachusetts
Harcourt Bindery
9-11 Harcourt Street
BOSTON
MA 02116
Tel. (617) 536 5755

New York
Center for Book Arts
15 Bleecker Street
NEW YORK
NY 10012
Tel. (212) 260 6860

There are many individual
teachers of bookbinding in the
US, and the student should
contact the Guild of Book
Workers (521 Fifth Avenue,
17th Floor, New York, NY
10175) for a list of addresses.

Societies

UNITED KINGDOM
Designer Bookbinders
6 Queen Square
LONDON
WC1N 3AR

The Society of Bookbinders
T. Walker Esq. (*National Chairman*)
12 Beckley Avenue
Prestwich
MANCHESTER
M25 8RR
Tel. (061) 773 4707

London and the South
K.C. Gostling Esq
5 Elsworthy
THAMES DITTON
Surrey
KT7 0YP
Tel. (01) 398 2481

The Midlands
R.H. Smith Esq.
Main Library
University of Birmingham
P.O.B. 363
BIRMINGHAM
B15 2TT
Tel. (021) 472 1301

The North West
Eric Pailin Esq.
43 Park Mount Drive
MACCLESFIELD
Cheshire
SK11 8NT
Tel. (0625) 23862

Wales and the West
Brian Edwards Esq.
60 Napier Road
Upper Weston
BATH
Avon
BA1 4LW
Tel. (0225) 25010

North Wales
P. Delrue Esq.
Studio 8
Ruthin Craft Centre
Park Street
RUTHIN
Clwyd
LL15 1BB
Tel. (08242) 4911

Scotland
J.E. McIntyre Esq.
40 Burghmuir Court
LINLITHGOW
West Lothian
EH49 7RS
Tel. (0506) 843116

USA
Guild of Book Workers
521 Fifth Avenue (17th floor)
NEW YORK
NY 10175
Tel. (212) 757 6454

Pacific Center for the Book Arts
157 Bluxome Street
SAN FRANCISCO
CA 94107

Hand Bookbinders of California
P.O. Box 3216
SAN FRANCISCO
CA 94116

Suppliers

UNITED KINGDOM
General bookbinding supplies
Falkiner Fine Papers Ltd
117 Long Acre
Covent Garden
LONDON
WC2E 9PA
Tel. (01) 240 2339

J. Hewit and Sons Ltd
97 St John Street
LONDON
EC1M 4AT
Tel. (01) 253 6082
(also at:
Kinauld Leather Works
Currie
EDINBURGH
EH14 5RS
Tel. (031) 449 2206)

Russell Bookcrafts
94 Bancroft
HITCHIN
Herts
SG5 1NF
Tel. (0462) 59711

Wooden equipment (nipping, lying and finishing presses, ploughs, sewing frames) made to order and repaired by:

The West Sussex Rural Engineering Co. Ltd
Charlton Farm
Charlton
SINGLETON
PO1 8HU
Sussex
Tel. (024 363) 762

Second-hand equipment
Falkiner Fine Papers (address as above)

Board, kraft, waxed and waterproof papers
A.J. Brown Brough and Co. Ltd
3 Dufferin Street
LONDON
EC1Y 8SD
Tel. (01) 638 8085

J. Hewit and Sons Ltd (address as above)

Machine-made, handmade, decorative and marbled papers
Falkiner Fine Papers Ltd
(address as above)
T.N. Lawrence and Son Ltd
2 Bleeding Heart Yard
Greville Street
LONDON
EC1N 8SL
Tel. (01) 242 3534

Russell Bookcrafts (address as above)

Paste, glue and PVA emulsions
Williams Adhesives Ltd
247 Argyll Avenue
SLOUGH
Berks
SL1 4HA
Tel. (0753) 24343/36496

Leather
Harmatan Leather
Unit J
Penfold Industrial Estate
Imperial way
NORTH WATFORD
Herts
WD2 4YY
Tel. (0923) 38453

J. Hewit and Sons Ltd, Russell Bookcrafts (addresses as above)

Finishing tools, type, handle letters, foils and nipping presses
John T. Marshall Ltd
Canonbury Works
Dove Road
LONDON
N1 3LY
Tel. (01) 226 7957

Russell Bookcrafts (address as above)

Gold leaf and foils
E. Ploton (Sundries) Ltd
273 Archway Road
LONDON
N6 5AA
Tel. (01) 348 0315

USA

General bookbinding supplies
TALAS
213 West 35th Street
NEW YORK
NY 10001-1996
Tel. (212) 736 7744

Basic Crafts Co.
1201 Broadway
NEW YORK
NY 10001
Tel. (212) 679 3516

Bookmakers
2025 Eye Street, NW
Room 502
WASHINGTON
DC 20006
Tel. (202) 296 6613

Harcourt Bindery
9-11 Harcourt Street
BOSTON
MA 02166
Tel. (617) 536 2755

Gane Brothers and Lane, Inc.
Mail Order Catalog Division
1400 Greenleaf Avenue
ELK GROVE VILLAGE
IL 60007
Tel. (312) 593 3360

Presses, tools
W.O. Hickok Manufacturing Co.
9th and Cumberland Streets

P.O. Box 2433
HARRISBURG
PA 17105-2433
Tel. (717) 234 8041

Paper
New York Central Supply Co.
62 3rd Avenue (11th Street)
NEW YORK
NY 10003
Tel. (212) 473 7705

Andrews/Nelson/Whitehead
31-10 48th Avenue
LONG ISLAND CITY
NY 11101
Tel. (212) 937 7100

Process Materials Corp.
301 Veterans Boulevard
RUTHERFORD
NJ 07070
Tel. (201) 935 2900

Board
The Davey Co.
164 Laidlaw Avenue
JERSEY CITY
NJ 07306
Tel. (201) 653 0606

Holliston Mills, Inc.
Customer Service
P.O. Box 478
KINGSPORT
TN 37662
Tel. (800) 251 0451
(Also sell coverings, reinforcement materials, headbands, foils.)

Bookcloth
Western Mills Co.
Industrial Products
220 Broad Street
KINGSPORT
TN 37660
Tel. (800) 251 7528
or (615) 247 2131

Holliston Mills, Inc. (address as above)

Adhesives
University Products, Inc.
P.O. Box 101
(South Canal Street)

HOLYOKE
MA 01040
Tel. (413) 532 4277

Process Materials Corp. (address as above)

Thread
University Products, Inc.
(address as above)

Leather
Andrews/Nelson/Whitehead
(address as above)

Leather-working tools
Henry Westpfal & Co., Inc.
4 East 32nd Street

NEW YORK
NY 10016
Tel. (212) 684 4687
(Also offers a sharpening service, and sells brushes and glue pots.)

Gold leaf
Wehrung and Billmeier Co.
3206 Southport Avenue
CHICAGO
IL 60657
Tel. (312) 472 1544

Gold foil
Kensol-Olsenmark, Inc.
40 Melville Park Road

MELVILLE
Long Island
NY 11746
Tel. (516) 694 7773

Holliston Mills, Inc. (address as above)

Books on printing, paper; private press imprints
Chiswick Book Shop
Walnut Tree Hill Road
SANDY HOOK
CT 06482
Tel. (203) 426 3220

Further Reading

Background
Brassington, William Salt, *A History of the Art of Bookbinding*, Elliot Stock, London, 1894, Macmillan, New York, 1893.

(An academic discourse on the development of the book and its decoration, from its origins to the late nineteenth century. Examples of modern bookbinding design may be found in the many catalogues and reviews published by the Designer Bookbinders, 6 Queen Square, London WC1N 3AR.)

Ede, Charles, *The Art of the Book*, Studio Publications, London and New York, 1951.

Poortenaar, Jan, *The Art of the Book and its Illustration*, Harrap, London, J.B. Lippincott, Philadelphia, 1935.

(These two volumes contain the essential background information on the artistic and technical achievements in book production.)

Middleton, Bernard C., *A History of English Craft Bookbinding Technique*, Hafner, New York and London, 1963.

(An excellent piece of research on the developing techniques of bookbinding through the centuries. Mr Middleton is the leading authority on technique, and this book is essential for the book restorer.)

Paper Making: A General Account of Its History, Processes and Application, British Paper and Board Makers' Association, Kenley (Surrey), 1949.

(A thorough and fascinating study of all aspects of paper-making.)

Printing Reproduction Pocket Pal, Advertising Agency Production Association, London, 1966.

(A pocket book which explains most of the technical processes associated with printing and book production that the bookbinder will meet with.)

Practical
Burdett, Eric, *The Craft of Bookbinding*, David and Charles, Newton Abbott, 1975, North Pomfret (VT), 1977

(A book of considerable merit as an instruction handbook, from a teacher of many years' experience. All binding operations are made clear by text, diagrams and photographs.)

Cockerell, Douglas, *Bookbinding and the Care of Books*, J. Hogg, London, Appleton, New York, 1901.

(A book which is itself part of the history of bookbinding, being the first instruction manual written for the amateur. Some of the operations are out of date and are described on the assumption that the reader has had some experience. Nevertheless a valuable contribution to a workshop library.)

Johnson, Arthur W., *Manual of Bookbinding*, Thames and Hudson, London, 1978, Thames and Hudson Inc, New York, 1981.

(Well-illustrated instruction book for the amateur and professional with some experience in bookbinding. It emphasizes the artistic aspect of the craft, and includes contemporary changes in book construction, box making and design not found in similar manuals.)